Brokenhearted
Ministering in Times of Loss

By Colquitt Nash

© 2025 Spiritbuilding Publishers.
All rights reserved. No part of this book may be reproduced in any form without the written permission of the publisher.

Published by
Spiritbuilding Publishers
9700 Ferry Road, Waynesville, Ohio 45068

BROKENHEARTED
Ministering in Times of Loss
By Colquitt Nash

ISBN: 978-1-964-80529-0

Spiritbuilding
PUBLISHERS

spiritbuilding.com

Table of Contents

Introduction 1
Chapter 1   Self-Awareness 3
Chapter 2   What Is Grief? 9
Chapter 3   Stages of Grief 17
Chapter 4   A Theology of Grief 22
Chapter 5   What Do I Do? 30
Chapter 6   What Do I Say or Not Say? 34
Chapter 7   Responding to a Death Call at the Hospital 39
Chapter 8   After the Funeral 43
Chapter 9   Sojourning with a Griever 47
Chapter 10   Talking to Help a Griever 53
Chapter 11   Helping the Griever Move Forward 58
Chapter 12   Ministering to a Family Following a Suicide ... 64
Chapter 13   Ministering to a Family After the Death of a Child ... 71
Appendix 1 78
Appendix 2   Steps for the Sojourning Process 83
Appendix 3   Grief and Assessment 85
Spiritual Assessment Tool for Crises and Grief 91
Appendix 4   A Guide for Those Helping Others with Grief ... 92
Bibliography/Resources 95

Introduction

News headlines and reports speak to us about death nearly every day. Whether it is a well-known person or people unknown to us, a single death or a multiple-death car wreck, the presence of death in this world cannot be denied. It can, however, be ignored.

Death seems to permeate our consciousness but not our conversation. Sometimes, we seem to have the child-like attitude that if something is not talked about, it really doesn't exist, or at least it won't happen to us. The anthropologist Margaret Mead is reported to have said, "When a person is born, we rejoice, and when they're married, we jubilate, but when they die, we try to pretend that nothing happened."

It is readily agreed that talking about death is not always pleasant or comfortable. Nevertheless, we must overcome our reticence to talk about it with one another, especially those close to us or those to whom we minister. Contrary to popular belief, there may not always be time to talk about death later. Death does not come only to those who are old, nor does it come only after a lengthy time of illness. The young die. Healthy people going about their lives meet with fatal accidents or suddenly contract terminal illnesses.

Considering that the latest research shows the mortality rate for the human race is 100%, one can only wonder why the topic of death is not discussed more. Perhaps that statement needs to be qualified. We do talk about death. We daily hear about murders and people killed in various other ways. What we do not talk about is our own death or those of our loved ones. Because these deaths are not discussed more, a couple of results seem to be experienced. First, we do not readily admit, accept, or prepare for our own deaths. Second, we do not know how to help those who are dying or console those who remain. The reality we need to embrace whether we think about our own death or the death of a loved one is this: death is a part of life.

That reality challenges those who have chosen to give their lives in church ministry. However, many do not feel adequate when confronted with ministering to families following a death. May some of the following thoughts help you as you touch the lives of those who grieve.

Chapter 1

Self-Awareness

Here is an interesting puzzle. In 1997, George Gallup surveyed 1,200 adults concerning the relationship between spiritual needs and the dying process. When the responses had been tallied:

- 54% said they would desire human contact as they were dying (others present)
- 47% would desire physical human contact (holding hands, etc.)
- 50% expressed a belief in the importance of prayer
- 44% indicated a desire for someone to help them achieve spiritual peace

For people in ministry, these percentages seem to indicate a time when those who serve in their respective faith communities would be welcomed and appreciated. However, only 36% of those surveyed felt that the presence of a minister would be comforting at that time.

When families or individuals are confronted with a terminal illness, many find themselves overwhelmed. Perhaps there are medical demands and decisions to be made. There may also be an accompanying burden of emotional and, in many cases, decision-making stresses. This has traditionally opened a role that ministers have filled.

However, many ministers—as well as many members of their congregations—do not feel comfortable participating in this role. In a study done in 1999 by Compassion Sabbath[1] related to the knowledge and attitude of ministers, only 37% of those surveyed said they minister *very effectively* to those who are seriously ill or dying. When asked if they were *very prepared* to minister to those who are seriously ill or dying, 44% replied affirmatively. When asked if the congregation *ministers very effectively*, only 18% agreed. 15% said their other staff or lay members were *very prepared* to do so.

Some ministers are not sure how to converse with the terminally ill or dying or with their families. They, too, can be overwhelmed by many issues surrounding the end of life. The daily demands of the minister's job responsibilities can hinder learning about such issues. At times, it even seems that the medical community marginalizes the minister's role in the situation. Not many ministers received any real training related to those who are terminally ill or dying in their preparatory studies. If they did, it may have been a very short period of instruction.

Caring for the dying and their families is challenging because there can be little tangible evidence that any good is being done. Yet it is this intangibility that makes the role of the minister so important in this process. Ministers should be those who are able to combine the mystery of spirituality with the desire to see purpose and meaning in life.

When you minister to a terminally ill or dying person, several others are also included. There is the family, the members of your congregation, friends, and even strangers. These people represent various cultural and personal attitudes that must be considered. Your attitude is also a variable in the mix and will affect how you minister in this arena.

Historically, death in America has been viewed as the greatest enemy of all humankind. Enemies are to be conquered. If the adversary cannot be vanquished, the result is that it becomes a hated thing, a terror to hide

---

[1] Compassion Sabbath is a national pilot program designed to provide tools and resources to help clergy meet the spiritual needs of seriously ill and dying people. The Compassion Sabbath concept grew out of a discussion between two pastors, Reverend Kelvin Calloway and Reverend Robert Lee Hill, who wanted to identify ways to help faith leaders ministering to the terminally ill in the Kansas City area.

from, to fear, to escape, to deny, and, whenever possible, to ignore. The problem, then, is based not so much on death and what it is as on death and how it is perceived.[2] Before going further into this discussion, it would be well for you to take some time and think about your answers to the following questions.

- What are your beliefs about life after death?
- Do you think it is appropriate for children to attend funerals?
- What most influenced your attitudes toward death?
- If you could choose, how would you die?
- How do you feel about having an autopsy done?
- What efforts should be made to keep a seriously ill person alive?
- What circumstances would prompt you to refuse or withdraw medical treatment for a dying family member?
- Are you willing to be an organ donor?
- If a close friend were dying and wanted to talk, how would you feel and what would you say?
- How do you want your body disposed of after death?
- What is your experience with various cultural rituals to remember the dead?

If those seem too heavy, here is another way to approach it:

1. I was first confronted with death at the age of _____ when my _____ died.

2. My reaction to my first confrontation with death was:
   a. sorrow
   b. loss, emptiness, loneliness
   c. lack of understanding, disbelief, confusion
   d. relief
   e. shock, fear
   f. other:

---

2   Rosalie Peck and Charlotte Stefanics, *Learning to Say Goodbye: Dealing with Death and Dying* (Muncie, Indiana: Accelerated Development, Inc. 1987), p. 3.

3. When I think of death now, I think of:
   a. loss—finality, loneliness, and/or separation
   b. sadness
   c. challenge, confusion, and/or inadequacy
   d. my own death
   e. relief to persons in pain
   f. selecting a method of dying, and/or support to the dying and their family
   g. a new life
   h. other:

4. If I learned today that I had a fatal illness, I would probably:
   a. be angry
   b. fall apart, be shocked, be confused, and/or be panic-stricken
   c. be able to accept the fact that I was dying
   d. not be able to accept the fact that I was dying
   e. be afraid
   f. not know what to do
   g. want to die immediately
   h. continue as normal
   i. fight to live
   j. other:

5. I would WANT my family to know I had a fatal illness because:
   a. I would want to help them to prepare for my death
   b. we could personally become closer
   c. we could prepare for our financial or business matters
   d. we could share our feelings and have emotional support for each other
   e. other:

6. I would NOT WANT my family to know I had a fatal illness because:
   a. I would not want them to feel sorry for me
   b. it would hurt them too much
   c. I would not want them to treat me differently because of sympathy or pity
   d. I do not want them to suffer or worry
   e. I would not want my family to change their patterns of life because of my dying
   f. I would want to accept it first
   g. other:

7. If I needed help in facing death, the person I would trust more than most would be my:
   a. spouse
   b. parents
   c. siblings
   d. other relative or friend
   e. religious professional
   f. medical professional
   g. other:

8. As death approached, I would want to be certain that:
   a. my family accepted my death
   b. my financial matters are in order
   c. I am at peace with God, and I am spiritually ready
   d. that I never give up fighting to live
   e. I am not alone
   f. I am personally prepared to accept my own death
   g. other:

It is not difficult to find resource materials on the kind of services that terminal patients need. It is more of a problem to find instructive information designed specifically to help you prepare yourself to meet the challenge of developing self-awareness, inner strengths and skills that are necessary for offering these unique, supportive services in terminal care.[3]

Knowing yourself will put you in a better position to support, comfort, and guide those you are called to minister. Even if you cannot provide all the answers, you will be a personal, caring, and comforting presence, which is the most important part of this process.

---

3   Peck and Stefanics, p. xii.

Chapter 2

What is Grief?

The first step to learning about anything is to define the topic. As Julie Andrews might say, "Let's start at the very beginning."[4] How do you define "grief"?

Some people assume bereavement is the same as grief. According to the dictionary, bereavement is defined as the state or fact of being bereaved (suffering the death of a loved one).[5] Grief, on the other hand, has been defined as the normal and natural reaction to loss of any kind and the conflicting feelings caused by the end of or a change in a familiar pattern of behavior.[6]

Grief is primarily an emotional reaction, but many try to treat it as an intellectual one. Although many try to handle their grief intellectually, they struggle to do so because the problem is not that they have a broken brain but a broken heart.

The emotions a person experiences during grief are varied and unpredictable as the following illustration[7] shows.

---

4   Richard Rogers and Oscar Hammerstein II, "Do-RE-Mi," 8th track on the original soundtrack of the Sound of Music, sung by Julie Andrews, produced by Neely Plumb, and released on March 2, 1965, by RCA Victor.

5   *Merriam-Webster's Collegiate Dictionary*, tenth edition (Springfield, Mass.: Merriam-Webster, Inc., 1999), p. 107.

6   John James and Russell Friedman, *The Grief Recovery Handbook: Twentieth Anniversary Expanded Edition* (New York: HarperCollins, 2009), p. 3.

7   Taken from H. Norman Wright, *Helping Those in Grief* (Ventura, CA: Regal, 2011),

Ball of Grief

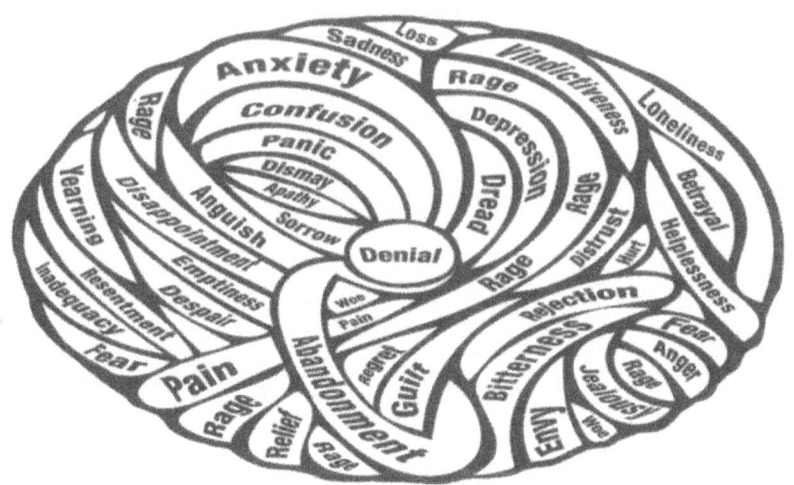

Grief also affects the whole person as illustrated below and as David said in Psalm 31:9—*Be gracious to me, O Lord, for I am in distress; my eye is wasted away from grief, my soul and my body also.* (NASB)

GRIEF AFFECTS THE WHOLE PERSON

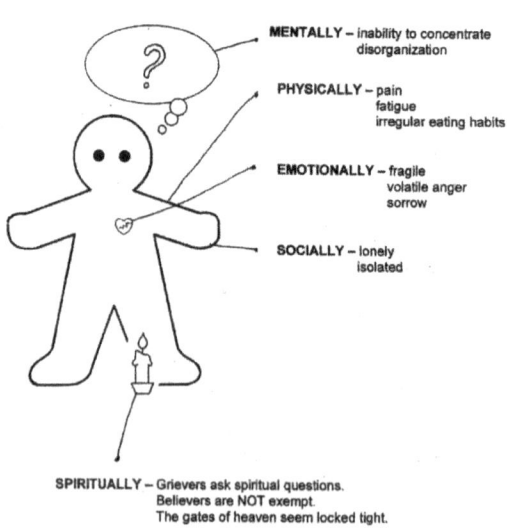

p. 114.

Grief has a way of skewing our emotions and perceptions—in a sense, making us "flat-brained."

Most of us operate with minds that are relatively open, receiving and processing information in a reasonable and rational way indicated in this illustration[8] by the square box in our head. Our hearts are open to receiving and giving love indicated by the heart with two sides. Our emotions are generally under control and not too disturbed by what is happening as indicated by the large circle in the gut area.

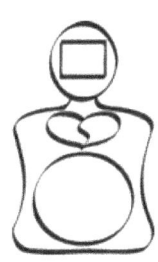

As children, all of these areas work well and seem to communicate with one another easily. By that, I mean children seem to be able to easily express what they are thinking and feeling. However, at some point in our development, we put a divider between our thinking and feeling. Everything still works like it should: our minds are reasonable and rational; we are able to give and receive love, and we still have emotional reactions. The problem is, for many of us, it becomes less easy to talk about or express our emotions, especially very intense and personal ones, like grief.

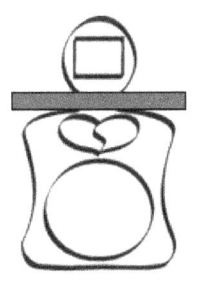

As we go through life, we experience losses, which, because of the emotional reaction to them, can be described as grief. Most of them are not life-changing and are easily handled. They do, however, stay with us as all our experiences do. They remain within but may not affect us to any great measure. Ashley Davis Bush described it this way:

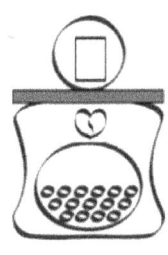

Your journey along the grief road actually began long, long ago, with your very first breath of life ... Every day thereafter, you have

---

8   These illustrations are adapted from Dr. Jim Petersen, *Why Don't We Listen Better?* (Tigard, OR: Petersen Publications, 2007) and used by permission.

experienced thousands of minor and major losses—from the loss of a bottle to the loss of a job, from the loss of your baby teeth to the loss of a friendship, from the loss of childhood innocence to the loss of adult dreams.

Every life transition, every beginning and ending you've ever experienced involved loss ... Effectively, they are grieving. Life is full of painful endings not related specifically to death, such as a job loss, an illness, a romantic breakup, or divorce, and each of these also requires a transition stage as the old is discarded and the new is formulated.

So, the truth is that, whether you realize it or not, you've actually been grieving on some level throughout your life. Clearly, some losses are more traumatic than others, and some are harder to adapt to, thus requiring more time and energy...That's why understanding the grieving process is critical since it is a relentless reality approaching every one of us at every turn in life.[9]

Although we have grieved at various times in our lives, we seem to get by very well. Then, one day, another grief event happens—one that is more intense than the others. Our emotional reaction to this event overwhelms our ability to handle these things. This flooding of our emotional space pushes against all that is around us. Pushing upward, it compresses our hearts into a brick that renders us incapable of giving or receiving love, isolating us from those around us. Not being restricted by the barrier we have created between our emotions and our intellects, it pushes upward, compressing our minds into the top of our heads, making us "FLAT-BRAINED."

As you can see by the line running through the middle of our eyes and ears, it affects what we hear and what we see and perceive. The only thing not apparently affected is our mouth. However, it is not fully connected to our brains, and we often say things that are not really from ourselves.

---

9 Ashley Davis Bush, <u>Transcending Loss</u>. (New York: Berkley Books, 1997), p. 3-4.

In this state, grievers may say things that surprise those around them. It is at this point grievers need to be heard, not challenged. The intensity will fade, and the griever will return to a place where their minds will process again, their hearts will love again and receive love from others, and their emotions will subside. The event, however, will remain as have all the others.

One of the key things you, as a minister, must share with those who are struggling with death or end-of-life issues is that what they are experiencing is NORMAL and NATURAL. Although our society and culture seem to ignore any *bad* feelings, such as grief, those feelings are there and are experienced by everyone at some level with varying levels of intensity. At times, some people will feel overwhelmed by these feelings. They need to be assured that they are not going crazy but are only experiencing what is normal and natural for them. Note some of these Crazy Feelings of Grief people might experience.

The Crazy Feelings of Grief

- Distorted thinking patterns, "crazy" and/or irrational thoughts, fearful thoughts
- Feelings of despair and hopelessness
- Out-of-control or numbed emotions
- Changes in sensory perceptions (sight, taste, smell, etc.)
- Increased irritability
- May want to talk a lot or not at all
- Memory lags and mental "short-circuits"
- Inability to concentrate
- Obsessive focus on the loved one
- Losing track of time
- Increase or decrease of appetite and/or sexual desire
- Difficulty falling asleep or staying asleep
- Dreams in which the deceased seems to visit the griever
- Nightmares in which death themes are repeated
- Physical illnesses like the flu, headaches, or other maladies
- Shattered beliefs about life, the world and even God

Taken from H. Norman Wright, *Helping Those Who Grieve* (Ventura, CA: Regal, 2011), p. 46.

Grief and its effects have been described as an ocean. There are waves and tides that rise and fall. Sometimes, there is relative calm, and at other times, there are heavy storms. One person has said that you cannot control the ocean, you can only learn to swim in it.[10] The one thing about grief is that it is unpredictable and different for every individual.

Having noted that grief is an emotional reaction, one must also be aware that some people try to process it intellectually. This may be due, in part, to the widespread belief and discussion about the Stages of Grief, which will be discussed in the next chapter.

Some talk about how men and women process grief differently. I believe it is more appropriate to talk about two different grieving styles: instrumental (intellectually) and intuitive (emotionally). Grief is as individual as each person's relationship to the person or loss. People may share similar events, such as the death of a mother, but that is simply an intellectual fact. The relationship between the person living and the person who died may be very different. All relationships are unique, no exceptions.[11] Therefore, each person grieves differently, whether a man or a woman. The following chart describes the two styles.

Instrumental Griever	Intuitive Griever
Focuses on cognitive thinking and thought processes	Focuses on feelings and emotions over thinking
Brief periods of cognitive dysfunction are common	Longer term of cognitive impairment; a feeling of disorientation or disorganization

---

10   Vicki Harrison

11   John James and Russell Friedman, *The Grief Recovery Handbook: Twentieth Anniversary Expanded Edition* (New York: HarperCollins, 2009), p. 40.

Instrumental Griever	Intuitive Griever
A desire to master the environment; to be in control of what is going on; most of one's energy is focused on problem-solving activity; planning activity is an adaptive strategy	Less likely to deal with problem solving; most of one's energy is focused on feelings and emotions; need time and space to feel and process emotions
Reluctant to talk about feelings	Feelings are intensely experienced
Grief is more an intellectual experience	Crying and lamenting mirror one's inner experience
May initially respond to the question "How are you doing?" by explaining the circumstances of the loss rather than express how one is feeling	When asked "How are you doing?" they may cry; response is related to feelings and emotions that are being experienced
May experience grief physically as restlessness or an abundance of nervous energy	May experience grief as physical exhaustion, and/or anxiety may be present
May be unaware of internal emotions	Aware of internal emotions, expressing them freely
Feels disenfranchised as others do not accept the fact you are grieving as they would expect you to do	Are fully into the grief experience
Uncomfortable with strongly expressed emotions by others	May be unable or unwilling to distance yourself from the feelings expressed by others

As stated earlier, a key task for you, as a minister, is to help a person or a family recognize what they are feeling is NORMAL and NATURAL. Realize that as a part of their grief, there may be anger toward:

- the situation of a person's death
- the person who died (if a suicide)
- the doctors (if a person doesn't think they did enough)
- themselves
- God
- the whole world in general

Your job is *not* to defend anyone. It is to be a safe sounding board. Grieving produces energy, and many times, that energy is released through talking and expressing some of the frustrations. Grievers may say things they normally wouldn't say. They might make statements that seem very different from the faith you know they have. They may have questions like:

- Why did this have to happen?
- How was this in God's plan?
- Where was God?
- How does any of this make sense?

This is not the time for a sermon. Do not chastise them for a lack of faith or trust in God. Listen to them with a big heart. As they process their grief, their anger will subside. They may even apologize to you later for some of their statements, and you will have an opportunity to encourage them in their growth. In a later chapter, we will look at the theology of suffering and what the Bible has to say about grief.

Chapter 3

Stages of Grief

You may be familiar with the Stages of Grief attributed to Elisabeth Kübler-Ross in 1969. She and her associates conducted a study on the reactions of terminally ill patients. Their conclusions were to define five stages related to their diagnosis:

- Denial
- Anger
- Bargaining
- Depression
- Acceptance

A simplistic way of illustrating these is seen as follows.

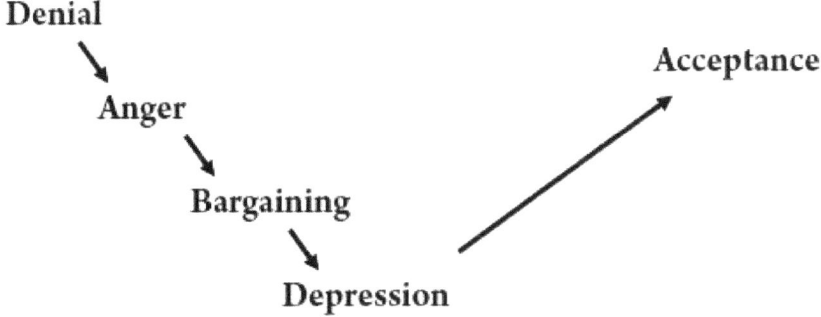

These five *stages* have been associated with grief by many people. In my opinion, this has led many people to believe that grief is a linear journey from point A to point B and is best dealt with intellectually. Also, these conclusions were about patients and not grievers. Not all of these describe grievers. For instance, I have never met a griever who denied that a loss had taken place. Not always is a griever angry. Grievers may wish things had been different, but do not bargain about that change. Depression may happen in some cases, but not always. As far as acceptance, it is most often simply a new normal.

Grief is not a linear journey; rather, it is a disorderly process. Some grief may be processed relatively quickly. Some grievers may spend more time in one area than others or may postpone some stages until a later time. It is a journey that may often wind back on itself time and time again. In the following illustration, the left-hand side is how many perceive the journey through grief. However, one griever has illustrated their grief journey on the right-hand side:

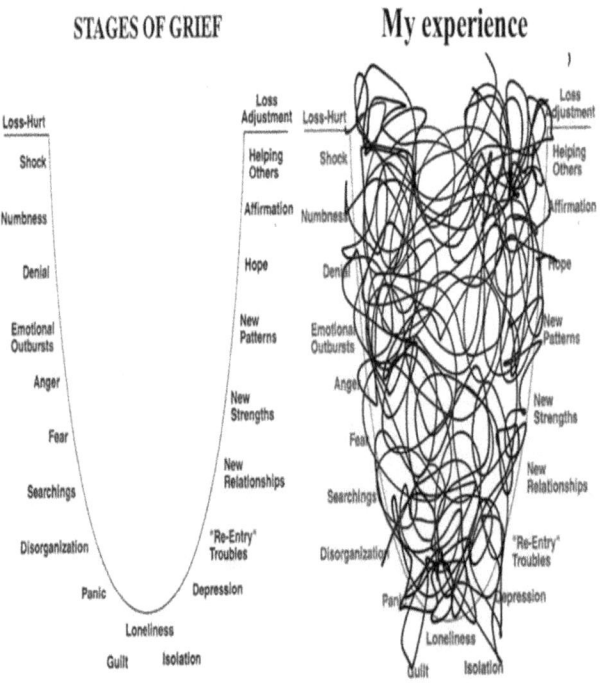

Instead of discussing the stages of grief, perhaps grievers would be better served by using the term phases of grief. Nearly every griever experiences seasons of grief, although not always in the same order or intensity. H. Norman Wright illustrates his conception of the phases of grief in this way.

The Normal Crisis Pattern[13]	Phase 1: Impact	Phase 2: Withdrawal/ Confusion	Phase 3: Adjustment	Phase 4: Reconstruction/ Reconciliation
Emotional Level				
Time:	Few hours to a few days	Days to weeks	Weeks to months	Months
Response:	Should I stay and face it or withdraw?	Intense emotions. You feel drained. Anger, sadness, fear, anxiety, depression, rage, guilt.	Your positive thoughts begin returning along with all emotions.	Hope has returned. Self-confidence.
Thoughts:	Numb, disoriented. Insight ability limited. Feelings overwhelm.	Thinking ability limited. Uncertainty and ambiguity.	You're now able to problem solve.	Thinking is clearer.
Direction You Take to Regain Control	You search for what you lost.	Bargaining/wishful thinking. Detachment.	You begin to look for something new to invest in.	Progress is evident and new attachments are made to something significant.
Searching Behavior	Often reminiscing.	Puzzled, unclear.	You can now stay focused and begin to learn from your experience.	You may want to stop and evaluate where you've been and where you're going.

The one negative aspect of this model is that there is NO timetable for grieving. As stated previously, some grievers will process their grief rather quickly, some may skip around, perhaps revisiting certain phases several times, and some may stay in one area for a long while. Every person grieves differently, making grief and how it is dealt with as individual as the person experiencing it.

Although some say grief generally lasts from 6 months to 4 years, a study published in the *British Journal of Psychiatry* suggested the intensity of grief peaked at 4 to 6 months and subsided during the next two years. Various cultures have formal mourning periods of time ranging from 1 year to 3 years. In the United States, a generally accepted time period is 1 year. However, most people find their hearts still hurt long after that time frame. Again, there is **NO** timetable for grieving.

In 2013, the DSM-5 (*Diagnostic and Statistical Manual of Mental Disorders*) changed its treatment of those expressing grief from the DSM-4 by proposing to exclude bereavement in its assessments and diagnosis. In essence, the new proposal labeled a newly bereaved person—within the first two weeks after the loss—as having a Major Depressive Episode (MDE) even though what they are experiencing is a normal reaction to the loss.

Interestingly, in March 2022, a revised version of the DSM-5 came out with a new yet debated and controversial diagnosis—prolonged grief disorder. According to Ellen Barry in her *New York* Times article "How Long Should It Take to Grieve? Psychiatry Has Come Up with an Answer,"

> The new diagnosis was designed to apply to a narrow slice of the population who are incapacitated, pining and ruminating a year after a loss, and unable to return to previous activities.

Depression was one of the characteristics Kübler-Ross found that was experienced by terminally ill patients. Grief sometimes has the appearance of depression, but it may not be. However, some physicians will prescribe anti-depression medications to those who are grieving. This may help in the short term, but in most cases, these medications will interfere with the grieving process.

One other thing to consider is how our culture generally assesses the time needed for a person to grieve. If an employee is injured in an accident or has surgery, they are generally given about 6 weeks for recovery. The law gives a woman giving birth a 3-month window to recover and adjust. Even fathers are allowed that same 3-month period. However, if an employee notifies his company of a death in the family, that employee is generally given about 3 days before they are expected back at their place and functioning as usual.

The crucial things then to remember are:

- Grief has no timetable. There are seasons or phases a person's grief may go through, but it hardly ever moves in a linear fashion so that, having passed through one point, that point will not show up again.
- Each person's grief is unique, and their recovery process is unique as well. Grievers must not be pushed to move faster than they should.
- There is **NO** timetable for grief.

Chapter 4

A Theology of Grief

The journey through life is a series of losses, crises and, in some cases, traumas—some are predictable and expected, but others are total surprises. Some crises are developmental; some are situational…Being alive means that we constantly have to resolve problems…One day, however, we will encounter a change or problem that seems beyond our capacity to cope. When a problem is overwhelming, or when our support system—within ourselves or from others—doesn't work, we are thrown off balance. This is called a *crisis*. Losses, crises, and traumas are part of life.

This can be devastating for a person without faith. However, the Bible provides a theological foundation for understanding the place of suffering in our world and in God's program, which secures and anchors those who find it and those who seek to help others.

Knowing and understanding the theological basis of suffering is important because the crises and the suffering that accompanies them can create some of the greatest challenges to faith that human beings experience. Note the following points:

1. Crisis and suffering are universal—Job 14:1 states that *man, who is born of woman, is short-lived and full of turmoil.*

2. Suffering involves the whole person; it is holistic in its impact.

3. Suffering leaves a person overwhelmed and weighed down by questions and pain—Ecclesiastes 1:14-15—*I have seen all the works which have been done under the sun, and behold, all is vanity and striving after wind. What is crooked cannot be straightened and what is lacking cannot be counted.*

Even knowing these things still causes us to ask, "Why?" and "What do I do?" Considering these truths about suffering, we must also be aware that neither simple answers nor quick fixes will work. Recovery from the grief associated with our losses is a process. Recognize, however, that when someone experiencing a crisis or grief comes to you, you are being given an opportunity to plant seeds of healing and growth.

When this opportunity is presented to you, there are however, two dangers:

1. If you are not careful and prepared, you may be pulled under. People who swim out to rescue a person flailing in the water must be careful not to be pulled under themselves by the very person they are trying to help.

2. The person being approached for help may feel as if they have nothing to offer.

We need to understand how crisis and suffering have impacted our own lives, how we have responded to it and moved on, and let God use us as instruments to help others.

2 Corinthians 1:3-4—*Blessed be the God and Father of our Lord Jesus Christ, the Father of mercies and God of all comfort, who comforts us in all our affliction so that we will be able to comfort those who are in any affliction with the comfort which we ourselves are comforted by God.*

Crisis and suffering are catalysts for change in our lives, and people are the catalysts for change in the lives of other people. People are the conduits through which God's Spirit can and does His work.

What Are the Keys to Understanding Suffering?

1. Suffering has a beginning and an end—Psalm 30:5—...*weeping may last for the night, but a shout of joy comes in the morning.*

2. Everyone must endure suffering at some point in time—Ecclesiastes 3:1-4—*There is an appointed time for everything. And there is a time for every event under heaven—a time to give birth and a time to die; a time to plant and a time to uproot what is planted. A time to kill and a time to heal; a time to tear down and a time to build up. A time to weep and a time to laugh; a time to mourn and a time to dance.*

3. Suffering is never wasted in God's plan, even if we cannot understand it. Jeremiah 29:11—*for I know the plans I have for you, declares the Lord, plans for welfare and not for calamity to give you a future and a hope.*

   Genesis 45:5, 7-8—*now do not be grieved or angry with yourselves, because you sold me here, for God sent me before you to preserve life... God sent me before you to preserve for you a remnant in the earth, and to keep you alive by a great deliverance. Now, therefore, it was not you who sent me here, but God....*

   Ecclesiastes 3:11—*He has made everything appropriate in its time. He has also set eternity in their heart, yet so that man will not find out the work which God has done from the beginning even to the end.*

4. Suffering is embedded in the human experience of this fallen world—Romans 5:12—*therefore, just as through one man sin entered into the world, and death through sin, and so death has spread to all men.*

5. God suffers.
   Hosea 3:1—*then the Lord said to me, Go again, love a woman who is*

loved by her husband, yet an adulteress, even as the Lord loves the sons of Israel, though they turn to other gods and love raisin cakes.

John 11:35—*Jesus wept.*

What Causes Suffering?

1. Sometimes, it is a discipline because of sin.

- It was in the case of David and Bathsheba—2 Samuel 12:10—*now therefore, the sword shall not depart from your house because you have despised Me and have taken the wife of Uriah the Hittite to be your wife.*

- In the case of Job, it was not.

    Job 1:1—*there was a man in the land of Uz whose name was Job; and that man was blameless, upright, fearing God and turning away from evil.*

    Job 42:7—*it came about after the Lord had spoken these words to Job, that the Lord said to Eliphaz the Temanite, My wrath is kindled against you and against your two friends, because you have not spoken of Me what is right as My servant Job has.*

2. Suffering may be a tool to break one's love of this world.

    Ecclesiastes 2:22-25—*for what does a man get in all his labor and in his striving with which he labors under the sun? Because all his days his task is painful and grievous; even at night his mind does not rest. This too is vanity. There is nothing better for a man than to eat and drink and tell himself that his labor is good. This also I have seen that it is from the hand of God. For who can eat and who can have enjoyment without Him?*

    Matthew 6:19-21—*do not store up for yourselves treasures on earth, where moth and rust destroy, and where thieves break in and steal. But store up for yourselves treasures in heaven, where neither moth nor rust destroys, and where thieves do not break in and steal; for where your treasure is, there your heart will be also.*

Matthew 6:33—*but seek first His kingdom and His righteousness, and all these things will be added to you.*

3. Suffering may sometimes come into a person's life to accomplish God's objective or to bring Him glory.

   2 Corinthians 12:7-9—*because of the surpassing greatness of the revelations, for this reason, to keep me from exalting myself, there was given me a thorn in the flesh, a messenger of Satan to torment me—to keep me from exalting myself! Concerning this I implored the Lord three times that it might leave me. And He has said to me, My grace is sufficient for you, for power is perfected in weakness. Most gladly, therefore, I will rather boast about my weaknesses, so that the power of Christ may dwell in me.*

   John 9:1-3—*as He passed by, He saw a man blind from birth. And His disciples asked Him, Rabbi, who sinned, this man or his parents, that we would be born blind? Jesus answered, It was neither that this man sinned, nor his parents; but it was so that the works of God might be displayed in him.*

4. Suffering may come because we isolate ourselves or feel abandoned.

   1 Kings 19:4—*he himself went a day's journey into the wilderness, and came and sat down under a juniper tree; and he requested for himself that he might die, and said, It is enough now, O Lord, take my life for I am not better than my fathers.*

   1 Kings 19:14—*then he said, I have been very zealous for the Lord, the God of hosts; for the sons of Israel have forsaken Your covenant, torn down Your altars and killed Your prophets with the sword. And I alone am left; and they seek my life, to take it away.*

5. Suffering may be a part of filling up that which is lacking in the suffering of Christ—Colossians 1:24—*no I rejoice in my sufferings for your sake, and in my flesh I do my share on behalf of His body, which is the church, in filling up what is lacking in Christ's afflictions.*

6. Suffering may result from the consequences of other people's choices, as David's suffering was due to Saul's wanting David dead.

7. Suffering may be due to error-based thinking; having unrealistic expectations of what we or God should do.

Although the causes of suffering in a person's life may come from a variety of sources, it is a reality of life. Whether you are the one suffering or you are walking with someone through suffering, one vital truth to remember is that God is sovereign over all things, including our suffering. In His love for us, He wants to turn what may seem to be a bad thing into something positive in our lives.

Before we move on, let's take a few moments and look at a few passages to see what the Bible says about grief. This will not be an exhaustive study, but just a few passages to help us see some aspects of grief from God's perspective. Following each passage are some comments I have gleaned from many different sources over the years. I am certain you, from your own personal study of Scripture, can add to this list for your encouragement and to be of comfort to those whom you will serve in their grief.

Proverbs 15:13—*a joyful heart makes a cheerful face, but when the heart is sad, the spirit is broken.*

Many proverbs are simply contrasts and comparisons. Here, it is between a happy heart and one burdened with sorrow or grief. This is much like what we have already noticed: grief affects the whole person. Many times, a person's face reflects what is going on inside of them. Just as happiness may come and go, times of grieving will also sweep over us at times. This is normal and natural. Sometimes, grievers feel as if they will never be happy again. However, the psalmist also says -- *...weeping may last for the night, but a shout of joy comes in the morning* (Psalm 30:5).

Isaiah 53:4—*surely our griefs He Himself bore, and our sorrows He carried...*

Many times, grievers feel isolated and alone, as if no one understands. We know there is One who understands because He has been there. Jesus, as a man, went through the feelings we experience. Hebrews 4:15 says about Jesus—*we do not have a high priest who cannot sympathize with our weaknesses, but One who has been tempted in all things as we are....* Jesus knew the grief of losing someone He loved as He wept with the sisters of Lazarus in John 11:35. He knew the feeling of loneliness as He prayed in the garden of Gethsemane. Thus, He is able to understand our feelings of loss and loneliness as He walks with us.

1 Corinthians 15:54-55—*but when this perishable will have put on the imperishable, and this mortal will have put on immortality, then will come about the saying that is written, "Death is swallowed up in victory. O death, where is your sting?"*

Our culture seems to see death as the period at the end of the sentence, the end with nothing beyond. Many times, in grief, it does seem as if our world has ended. God's word promises that death is not the end, a period; it is only a comma, a pause for a while until that which God has prepared for His people will become a reality.

Philippians 3:13-14—*I do not regard myself as having laid hold of it yet; but one thing I do: forgetting what lies behind and reaching forward to what lies ahead, I press on toward the goal of the prize of the upward call of God in Christ Jesus.*

Some grievers may fear that if they let go of their grief, they will *forget* the one who has died. We can never forget. Relationships do not end; they simply change. A person may no longer be physically present, but they are present with us emotionally. However, grief may sometimes cause grievers to feel as if they are inside a house watching life go on around them for everyone else. As a person moves through the process of grief, there will come a time when they will re-engage in life—perhaps not in the way they once did, but with much of the same energy. We do not forget, but we keep going.

1 Thessalonians 4:13—*but we do not want you to be uninformed, brethren, about those who are asleep, so that you will not grieve as do the rest who have no hope.*

Many people are uninformed about grief because they have been taught and seen things modeled that are not true. Some have no relationship with God or with Jesus and will struggle with grief because, for them, there is nothing but despair beyond this life. For those people, the help you may be able to give is to encourage them to move beyond this difficult time to a different place. For those who do have a relationship with God and Jesus may only need to be reminded of the hope, strength, and comfort they have at their disposal through God's Spirit and the promises of His word.

Chapter 5

What Do I Do?

Knowing about grief is one thing; being able to help grievers is another. One thing to understand fully within yourself is that you will never be all you want to be or all the people you serve need you to be. Contrary to some of our own thoughts, none of us can step into a phone booth and fly out to save the world. We are all human. Only God can fulfill the needs we have. As ministers, we are only tools God may use. You must not take it personally if the help you offer is rejected or you are rebuffed. Remember, grief has a way of skewing our emotions and perceptions as we talked about being "flat-brained." Below are some suggestions for how you might respond to someone you may meet in this emotional state.

1. Sometimes, when people are first experiencing grief and those crazy feelings are overwhelming them, they will ask, "How could God let something like this happen?" They might even feel they are losing their faith. A good response is to just listen and reflect. "You are right; what has happened doesn't make much sense. I wish I had a good answer for you." Let them know these feelings are natural and normal. As the wise man of Proverbs said:

   The heart of the righteous ponders how to answer—Proverbs 15:28

   Oil and perfume make the heart glad, so a man's counsel is sweet to his friend—Proverbs 27:9

2. If the person says or shares something that shocks you, don't respond immediately and do NOT say, "You shouldn't say things like that." If you are caught off-guard and don't know what to say, ask for more information—"Tell me about that," or "Let me take a few seconds to go through what you just said and decide what thoughts I should share with you." Remember the words of Proverbs:

   … he who restrains his lips is wise—Proverbs 10:19

   A man has joy in an apt answer, and how delightful is a timely word—Proverbs 15:23

3. Don't try to come in and be a ray of sunshine—Proverbs 25:20—*like one who takes off a garment on a cold day, or like vinegar on soda, is he who sings songs to a troubled heart.*

4. You are not there to give them answers or advice. However, if they ask for advice, give tentative suggestions by saying, "What if you did _____?" or "Have you considered _____?" or "What ideas/possibilities have you thought about?" Walk beside them, helping them process some of these things rather than taking them by the hand and leading them.

5. If you must confront them, confront them in love. "I wonder if that is the best thing," or "Does that make sense to you?" Proverbs 17:10 says—*a rebuke goes deeper into one who has understanding than a hundred blows into a fool.*

6. Should they say, "I need your help," you need to find out what they mean. "What help can I give?" Help them in the things that may be overwhelming them, but do not take everything away from them. Galatians 6:2 tells us to bear one another's burdens (those things that overwhelm us), but Galatians 6:5 says we must each bear our own load.

7. Encourage them.

8. Above all, *keep confidences confidential!*

Other items to consider when thinking about what to do or not do:

1. Do not avoid the individual because you don't know what to do or say.

2. Do not avoid mentioning the deceased person's name.

3. Do not change the subject if they start talking about the deceased person or their death.

4. Do not force them to forgive, even if that is something needed. That may come as they process their grief, but it may also interfere with their recovery.

5. Give them the freedom for anger and questions. Do not prevent them from asking questions or being angry with God. At this point, they may not be thinking rationally and may say things they do not mean.

6. Do try to project yourself into their situation and how you would want to be treated or spoken to. (Matthew 7:12)

7. Give them the freedom to cry.

8. Offer tangible and practical ways you can help. People often say, "Let me know if there is anything you need done or I can help with." Grievers may not be able to think about things like that. Instead, offer something specific, such as cleaning the house, shopping for groceries, etc.

9. Remember them after the initial rush of the death and funeral/memorial. Although there is generally a rush of activity soon after a death and people surrounding the griever, when the dust has settled, and family and friends have settled back into their routines, the griever is often left alone. Send cards. Call and visit them. It is in this loneliness they need your presence.

Chapter 6

What Do I Say or Not Say?

As a minister, your heart is to help those who need help, to speak words of comfort and encouragement. There is, however, also a need for the ministry of presence—simply being there for another person as Job's friends were in the beginning (Job 2:11–13). There are times to speak words that are apples of gold in settings of silver (Proverbs 25:11) and that are good for the moment, giving grace to those who hear (Ephesians 4:29). There is also a time for silence (Ecclesiastes 3:7). Sometimes, I fear, we may rush in thinking we have to say something and begin speaking without having thought about our words. The stock answers we have been given are not what need to be heard. Words from our hearts to theirs are needed.

A study done years ago determined that, after a person loses a loved one to death, within about 72 hours, they will hear around 141 basic statements from those who share their condolences with them. Of those 141 statements, only 19 were truly helpful. It is not that people intentionally say things to grievers that do not help. People truly want to help, and they do it in the ways they have been taught or seen modeled.

What Should Not Be Said—Here are some things that one should never say to a griever.

1. "I know how you feel."

    In reality, we don't know how they feel. Each person's grief is as individual as their relationship was to the one who died. Siblings do not have the same feelings regarding a parent. Grief is an emotional experience. We sometimes continue our statement by saying something like, "My mother also died." That is an intellectual statement of fact. Both of you may have had mothers who died, but your feelings do not equate to their feelings, nor do theirs equate to yours. The only thing each of us can know is how we feel or felt when we experienced our own loss.

2. "It was just God's will." "They were such a good person, God wanted them to be in heaven."

    Again, this is an intellectual statement intended to help an emotional event. Although intended to bring comfort and encouragement to a person of faith, the implication that God caused their pain because of His desires may also cause them to struggle.

3. "They are in a better place." "They lived a good, long life."

    Intellectual, not emotionally helpful.

4. "You can still have another child."

    This is often said to younger couples who have had miscarriages or stillborn children. It also is an intellectual statement that does nothing to help the heartache of the moment.

There are times when a person has been grieving for a while following a death. As they are trying to process their grief and find direction, they also will hear statements that are not helpful.

1. "You need to keep busy."

    This is one of the myths about grief we have been taught. While it is true that busyness does take our minds off the pain of grief we may be experiencing, we cannot stay busy 24/7/365. At points when we slow down, grief catches us again.

2. "It just takes time."

   This is also true; however, time ALONE will not heal. If someone fell and broke their arm, would you say, "Don't worry. Just wrap it up, and in time it will be okay"? Time will heal the arm if it is properly set and cared for. Suppose you went to your car and found a flat tire. Would you just pull up a chair and tell anyone who asked, "If I wait long enough, time will put air back in my tire"? We all know that time will fix the flat if we change the tire or call someone to help. Time and action bring results, not time alone.

3. "Get yourself together. You should be over that by now."

   Remember, grief has no timetable. Each person processes grief differently and works through it on their own schedule. Statements like this sometimes cause grievers to feel what they are experiencing is not normal and may try to act the way people think they should. This may stall their grief recovery. Grievers should never be blamed for how they feel. Grievers do not need to be *fixed*.

What Should Be Said? Although no one thing is the right thing to say to a griever, here are some suggestions.

1. As mentioned at the beginning of this chapter, sometimes nothing needs to be said. Just being there can be a comforting gift to a person who is hurting.

2. "I heard what happened, and I don't know what to say."

3. "I am sorry for your loss. I can't begin to know how you feel."

4. If you knew the person who died, you might say, "When I thought about ____, I always thought about how ____." "One of my favorite memories about ____ is ____. I will miss them, too."
   Most of the time, you will be aware of the circumstances related to a person's loss. Should you be called into a situation where you may not be familiar with those circumstances, consider the following.

As soon as possible, ask, "What happened?"

1. If not addressed in their response, ask, "How did you find out?"

2. If it results from a long-term illness, you might ask, "When did you realize the seriousness of the situation?" and "Did you talk to anyone about it?"

3. "When did he or she first realize the seriousness of the situation? Did you talk to them about it?"

4. "Did you talk to anyone about your thoughts and feelings regarding the illness or the treatment?"

5. "Were you able to talk to them about their illness or treatment?"

6. "Did it help you?" "Did it help them?"

7. "Did anything happen in the final days or hours that still troubles you?"

8. "Do you remember the last conversation you had with them?" "What stands out for you in that last conversation?"

9. If you are visiting with the griever after a funeral or memorial has occurred, ask,
"Did anything happen or not happen at the funeral or memorial that troubles you?" or "In the days and weeks following your loss, did you have difficulty with anything said to you by friends, family, clergy, funeral personnel, or others?"

It is normal and natural for people following a loss to think about and review the relationship they had with the person who died. In that review, they will probably remember things they wish had ended differently or things that had been done more often. They will also remember things they wish they had said or done differently or more often, as well as things the other person had said or done differently or more often. The Grief Recovery Institute has developed the Grief Recovery Method, which helps people work through these things to become emotionally complete with the relationship. There are trained specialists through the Institute who can help people do this.

One final thought. Grievers need to tell their story. Be a heart with big ears when they need to talk. Encourage them to talk and listen to them.

Chapter 7

Responding to a Death Call at the Hospital

Suppose you are a minister who is serving as a volunteer chaplain at your local hospital, and you are called in response to a patient's death, and the doctor would like for you to be there when they talk to the family. Perhaps you are called by a family member or friend of one of your congregants to come to the hospital because they have just been involved in an accident and probably won't make it, and the family wants you to be there. What should you do? The following thoughts are basically for volunteer chaplains but will also pertain to a minister called to be there for a congregant.

Upon your arrival, you should find someone on the medical staff and ask them what has happened. You will need to know who it is, if you do not already, know what the circumstances are, what family members are present, and where they are. As you find them, introduce yourself to those you don't know.

Upon entering the room, look around at those there and seek out the calmest individual. Make eye contact and engage them in conversation. If you are not their minister, ask if they have a church they regularly attend and if you could contact that minister. Ask how they are related to the patient. Write down names as you are introduced. Ask, "What happened?"

Be prepared for varying responses. These folks are in the initial phase of grieving, and there may be numbness, disbelief, irrational thinking, etc. Also, remember that people will all grieve differently. Some will be stoic, others will be sobbing, and others will seem indifferent. As you proceed, offer to say a prayer or share a Scripture.

Be aware of other needs, such as offering to get water, tissues, or other things that might be needed. As a volunteer chaplain or minister, you are a liaison between the family and the hospital staff. Talk to the medical staff and pass along information to the family or take questions from the family to the medical staff.

This is a crucial time for your ministry of presence. Listen to the family, be close to them, encourage them, and seek to calm an anxious time. As much as possible, be a quiet, godly presence.

Be aware that if the family is separated from their loved one (they are in a family room, and the patient is in another room), the family will nearly always want to see their loved one, especially if they have died. When you can, escort them to the room and simply be a presence with them. You may offer to lead a prayer. If the loved one was in a serious accident and is very disfigured, you may want to dissuade the family from viewing the body. However, they may insist. At that point, you will especially need to be present with them when they see the body.

Family members will have many questions, among them, "Why?" Do not pretend to know the answer or give a stock answer such as, "It was God's will." It is not your place to stand in for or defend God. Simply acknowledge there are many things we cannot know that do not seem to make sense.

If the conversation seems to stop, do not feel like it is your job to keep it going. Allow the silence to give time for the people there to process what has happened. It is not your place to share any similar experiences you may have had. As God's ambassador, listen with your ears and heart to their grief. Allow them to talk if they want to because grievers need to tell their stories.

Do not be offended if the family declines your services or presence. If the family's minister was called, when he arrives, excuse yourself. Take this time to check on the hospital staff who may have ministered to the patient. These folks will also be grieving in their own way. Be a presence for them. One exception to leaving could be if this person's death were related to a major trauma. As the family's minister helps them, you may still be able to be a liaison between hospital staff and the family.

If you are serving as a volunteer chaplain, you may choose to leave if things seem to be going well. Inform the hospital staff, telling them to call you again if needed.

There are certain situations of which you should be aware. You might also talk to someone in your local area about these. For instance:

1. If it is an unexpected death, generally, the coroner will be called in to investigate and may have to release the body before the family can view it. In certain instances, bodies are sent to a state lab before being released.
2. If it is a motor vehicle accident or shooting, the coroner and the police will be involved. In such cases, the police generally will want to interview the family.
3. If it is the death of a child, Child Protective Services may be called in if there are suspicious circumstances. Again, the family will be interviewed.

Although you will be with the family, you are a NEUTRAL person in these circumstances. As such, allow the authorities the space they need to do their job. You have no comments to make.

At times, you may be called upon to deal with crowd control. If the family is using the hospital's family room, there may be more family than it will comfortably hold. Should this happen, check with the nurse in charge and ask if there is another location to which the family could be moved and encourage the family and others to go there. Find a family member who seems to be the leader and explain what needs to be done. If there is no other place, you should limit those in the family room only to IMMEDIATE family. If the family and others are non-compliant with these requests, you may have to have hospital security called in to help.

As mentioned above, the family members are not the only people to serve. Be mindful of the hospital staff—especially those attending to the patient. This is especially true during very traumatic events, the death of a child or young person or a tragic death. Be a ministry of presence for them. Find them and ask how they are feeling about what happened. You might ask them how they process or decompress from times like this. Listen to them; encourage them. Be aware that because they know who you are, they may seek you out.

These are the times you, as a person who cares about people, will be called upon to be ready to offer your care and compassion to those who need you. May God strengthen you to accomplish His will for you and those you serve.

Chapter 8

After the Funeral

What has been discussed thus far is just the proverbial tip of the iceberg. The initial encounter with a griever through whatever circumstance brought about their loss is an integral part of your ministry whether they are one of your congregants or not. For those who are not, hopefully, your presence was a calming influence at a chaotic time. For those who are your congregants, your ministry is to continue to walk with them through their grief journey.

Since most ministers have experience facilitating a funeral or memorial service, we will not spend much time with that. The point that will be discussed is the ongoing grief work after the funeral or memorial service. It is here, when the relatives and family have gone, when friends and others have returned to their regular routines, that the griever is often left alone to deal with life.

It is hoped that you, as a minister, recognize this as part of the spiritual work to which you have been called and committed. Grief work IS spiritual work as Carole Carson noted, "Because significant loss challenges an individual's core understanding of the meaning of life." In a 1999 report from the Fetzer Institute, a foundation using its resources to build a spiritual foundation for a loving world, this definition was given for the word *spirituality*:

Spirituality is concerned with the transcendent, addressing ultimate questions about life's meaning, with the assumption there is more to life than what we see or fully understand.

Perhaps that can be boiled down to say that the primary function of spirit and spiritual activity during grief is to make sense of loss and address the changed relational reality.

We, as human beings, are designed for relationships. Those relationships are attachments we have to people, things, or dreams. Those attachments can be physical, emotional, social, or mental. When those people or things are taken from us, we grieve. When our dreams and the expectations of the past, present, or future come to an end, we grieve. Our world is changed. Our present is different. Our future is uncertain. Although we recognize that every person's life and the relationships associated with life will have good times and losses, we seem to believe we will be the exception.

Grief or loss does shake a person's life. Recall that one of the definitions given for grief is the conflicting feelings caused by the end of or a change in a familiar pattern of behavior. This grief moves them into an area that may be unfamiliar. It may also be an area in which they are unprepared and causes them to question many things they have believed. Thus, as stated earlier, grief affects the whole person, including the spiritual side, which may cause a griever who is a believer to question God's power, compassion, or even His existence.

When grief upends the balance of a person's life, life's response is to work toward restoring that balance. When loss breaks the connectedness a person has to another person, thing, or dream, life's response is to seek reconnection. However, the new attachments and connections will not be the same as the old ones, yet they are the experiences of recovery and moving forward with life.

Remember that grief is not the same for every person. Grief is as individual as the griever's relationship was to their loss. For instance, if siblings lose a parent to death, each sibling's grief will be different because of their individual relationship with that parent. Also, a griever's response to recovering from grief is unique to them.

There are some similarities that are common to all grievers. First, grief is normal and natural. Grievers need to be assured of this often, as grief can be overwhelming at times. Second, grief takes time—not time alone, but time to work through what is happening to and within them.

As grievers tend to isolate, one task as a minister is to encourage your church family to continue reaching out to those who are grieving. This can be done by phone calls and visits. They need to be invited to join in activities. They should not be forced into them, but let them know about what is happening and make sure they know they are welcome. You may think they would know they are invited; however, many times, grievers feel like life is moving on around them as if they are watching through a window but not being a part of what is happening.

Grievers are not broken people. They are people with broken hearts. Thus, they do not need to be fixed by advice, no matter how well-meaning that advice may be. Neither do they need to be treated as exceptions. We are all on or will be on the same journey as they are at some point. Grievers need to be loved, remembered, and listened to.

Grievers need to tell and re-tell their story. People who work with grievers need to become hearts with big ears who listen attentively, and perhaps often, to what they are saying. Everyone has a story that needs to be told and heard. Often, griever's stories will begin with a phrase like, "I was all right until. ..." As a rule of thumb, people who have had significant losses tell stories of loss, grief, and their attempts to recover ... there is much drama and passion in the story, even if the feelings are repressed.

A part of the storytelling on the part of grievers may be due to the normal, human tendency to review and think through the relationship and/or the expectations which have now changed. Consider Luke's account of the two disciples on the road to Emmaus following the death and resurrection of Jesus in Luke 24. Luke recorded these disciples were *talking about the things which had taken place* (v. 14). The account goes on to relate to the events which had happened and the expectations they had held about Jesus. On top of all that, they were trying to make sense of the women who had brought the message of the resurrection.

In a griever's review, good things will be remembered. Challenging things may be identified. Hurts may be expressed. This review and storytelling help a griever process the feelings they are experiencing and the thoughts that fill their minds. Those listening should listen with respect and not judgment. Realize, too, that some of these thoughts and feelings may be compounded by previous losses that were not dealt with and are resurfacing in this loss. Thus, the task of those helping grievers is to walk with them as Jesus did those disciples and help them find reconnection and completeness.

Chapter 9

Sojourning with a Griever

Junietta Baker McCall wrote:

> Grief has frequently been described as a journey. In using this combination of symbol and imagery the person experiencing loss is imagined as going from one place to another and then returning or ending up somewhere else. Journeys can be unexpected, spontaneous, desired and undesired, prepared for and catch us unprepared. In this sense, journey is a wonderful image for the grief experience because it presents the basic healing context for grief's story to be told.

It may also be helpful to think about moving through grief as a process. Processes, like journeys, have beginnings, middles, and endings. Process also carries with it the idea that there are doable components that move toward completion. John James and Russell Friedman wrote, "Recovery from loss is achieved by a series of small and correct choices made by the griever."

A griever rarely thinks that the word *recovery* is something that will happen. Grievers need to be assured that they can move beyond their loss. This moving beyond does not mean they will ever forget or get over that loss. They will, rather, be able to continue living without being stuck in sadness or hurt. As you minister to those who are grieving, your task is to walk with them through this journey and help them to make those small and correct choices—to become a sojourner with them in their journey through grief.

You, as the minister and perhaps several other people close to the griever, may become the support system they need. When someone has suffered a loss and grief sets in, that person often feels devastated and alone. Many folks around the griever may avoid this person, not because they do not care but because they do not feel confident about what they should say or do. Hopefully, as you move through this study, you will feel confident in using these tools and suggestions to bring help and hope to those who grieve.

Perhaps we should start by first asking, "What is a sojourner for a griever?" Tim VanDuivendyk defined a sojourner as *one who intentionally supports a grieving person through the wilderness of grief.* The operative words might be *intentionally* and *supports*.

Another question might be, "What does it take to be a sojourner?" I am convinced there are several qualities a sojourner must have.

The first of those qualities is empathy. This is not sympathy. Empathy is feeling **WITH** another person and not **FOR** them. Empathy is the capacity of one person to enter another person's frame of reference, perspective, thoughts, and feelings as if it were their own. It is walking in another's shoes. It is to be with another person in their pain without trying to take that pain away. Carl Rogers expressed it in these words:

> …entering the private perceptual world of the other and becoming thoroughly at home in it. It involves being sensitive, moment by moment, to the changing felt meanings which flow in this other person, to the fear or rage or tenderness or confusion or whatever that he or she is experiencing. It means temporarily living in the other's life, moving about in it delicately without making judgments.

To accomplish this, one must take time to listen. Again, become a heart with big ears, listening without judgment and with patience. When talking to a griever, it may take them 4 to 9 seconds longer to respond to you than might otherwise be normal. But being empathetic is not simply being silent.

When talking with a griever, use feeling words and seek to elicit feeling responses such as, "You mean it feels like ____?" Use open-ended questions rather than simple yes or no answers such as, "How are you feeling?" instead of "Are you feeling okay?" You may also repeat the word(s) expressed by the griever—"It's like living in a fog?"

Sometimes, empathy is simply being wounded healers who have walked in similar circumstances to the griever and can offer hope. As the Holy Spirit shared through Paul in 2 Corinthians 1:3-4—*Blessed be the God and Father of our Lord Jesus Christ, the Father of mercies and God of all comfort, who comforts us in all our affliction so that we will be able to comfort those who are in any affliction with the comfort which we ourselves are comforted by God.*

Sojourners are people who love and communicate love. 1 John 3:18 says *let us not love with word or with tongue, but in deed and truth.* Therefore, sojourners make time for others as well as make time to care for themselves. Sojourners keep caring, although not always perfectly. They value the story of the griever without trying to inject their own stories. Sojourners invite grievers to express their feelings of fear, anger, sadness, and anxiety *without judging* the griever. Sojourners pray with and for grievers.

Those sojourning with grievers should not feel they must take charge of things even when the initial grief is intense enough to almost incapacitate the griever. A sojourner walks with a griever and not for them. There are times when those who care may need to help, but before taking action ask yourself these questions:

1. Is this something the griever could do for themselves?
2. If I do this, what will it accomplish in the long run?
3. How long would I need to be involved in this way?
4. Could the griever be helped in a different way?

Another key consideration is to ask yourself, "How much action should I take?" A rule of thumb might be to act only if circumstances severely limit the griever's ability to perform the needed task. That is not to say you could not do some chores around their house, take them shopping, or bring in meals. What it does is help them maintain a feeling of competence and responsibility and not create a feeling of dependency.

Never underestimate the power of your presence in the life of a griever. Simply remember that your part in this chapter of their lives is to support them—not to be their solution. As a sojourner, you will walk with them as they come to healing and recovery. The way may be difficult and filled with emotion, but it is God who is the strength and comfort they should come to know.

When talking with a griever, it is important to foster hope and positive expectations in their minds. Do not make false promises, but encourage them to think about their situation and come up with options. Your belief in this person's capability will be important for them.

The following is a distillation of things TO DO and NOT TO DO:

1. Don't minimize the griever's pain by saying, "It was probably for the best," "Things could have been worse," or "Remember that God is in control." These may appear to comfort, but they do not acknowledge the griever's pain or loss. Instead, offer simple understanding statements like, "I feel for you during this difficult time" or "I share your feelings of loss."
2. Don't say, "I'm sorry," and simply end the sentence. Say, "I'm sorry," but then add something like, "I know how special they were to you" or "I will miss them also".
3. Don't just say, "Is there anything I can do to help?" Ask the more open-ended question, "How can I help you right now?" or offer specific ways of helping such as, "What can I pick up for you at the store (or wherever)?" or if there are children involved, "Can I take the kids for a little while tomorrow afternoon?"
4. Don't say, "You shouldn't feel that way," or "Don't feel bad...." Encourage them to express their feelings or even write them down so they can better deal with them.
5. Don't change the subject if they begin talking about their loss. Allow them to speak even if it is uncomfortable for you. This is for their

comfort and recovery. Also allow them to express their pain through tears.
6. Don't try to answer the question, "Why?" Very simply, no one may have that answer. Instead, say, "I don't know why."
7. Don't offer clichés or comfortable spiritual answers that tend to all say, "You will be stronger or better after you get through this." Respond by saying, "What happened doesn't seem fair, and it is hard to make sense out of it." You, and they, may have an underlying belief that God can and will work everything for our good (Romans 8:28) and that He will give us the resources to make it through whatever comes (1 Corinthians 10:13), but during this hurt, pain has a way of eclipsing faith, although faith will eventually triumph.
8. Don't put timetables on the griever's recovery. Allow the person the time to deal effectively with their grief.
9. Don't simply quote Bible verses to comfort or minimize their pain as if those verses will bring them the help they need. Bible verses are rich sources of comfort and help, but share them by saying, "I have found this to be of help for me when I have struggled with …" Allow the scriptures to do their work (Hebrews 4:12). If you pray for them and they know you are praying, occasionally ask what you can specifically pray about for them.
10. Don't say, "I understand," even if you have faced the same situation. Don't say, "I know how you feel," because each person's grief and relationship to the loss is unique and individual. If you have not had a similar experience, say, "I can only imagine how you must feel." If you have had a similar experience, say, "I can remember how I felt when …"
11. Don't forget the person after the immediate rush of the event has passed. Keep in touch for months following. If the grief is because of the death of a loved one, be especially mindful of "special days" such as a birthday or an anniversary.
12. Don't be silent or wait until you can think of the perfect thing to say. If you do not know what to say, try, "I wish I knew what to say. I want you to know that I am thinking of you (or praying for you) and am here for you." If you cannot be with them or think of anything else to do, send a card or a note.

13. Don't use "should" or "if only"—"You should move/clean out the closet/go back to work or find a job." "If only they had (or you had)…" Allow hurting people to make their own decisions. These thoughts are already in their minds. They do not need others to add to their burden.

A spin-off of the previous thought would be, don't offer unasked-for advice. If the griever does ask your advice, respond cautiously and prayerfully. Advice needs to be couched in terms of "What if you were to _____ ?" or "Have you thought about _____ ?" Help the griever find their own answers.

Chapter 10

Talking to Help a Griever

As we have shared, grievers want and need to tell their stories, especially as they review their relationships within their minds. Grievers also tend to withdraw and isolate. For those close to the griever, this sometimes becomes a confusing paradox. Without being pushy, those who care for and minister to grievers need to continue to reach out to them and invite them to talk. Should you be one of those who care about a grieving person and yet see them struggling, here are some suggestions to help keep this process open.

Do not be afraid to talk to them about what you notice or feel in your relationship with them. You might say, "It seems to me there are some things bothering you. What's on your mind?" Allow this to be your invitation for them to talk about what is going on in their lives. Simply ask the question and wait. Be aware they might say, "Nothing," as they might feel they do not want to burden anyone with their problems. Allow that to be okay. Leave them with this encouragement, "Please know that if you do need someone to talk to, I am here." Then, make sure you are available to them when the time comes.

If they do share something, thank them for the courage to share with you and make any other appropriate response, such as, "I can only imagine how that is affecting you." Be aware that grievers will sometimes give an answer they feel they should, but it may not really be what is on their minds. If they give you an answer, you may also respond, "And what else?" Again, ask and wait. Do not push forward with other questions or qualifications of the question like, "It just seems there is more than that."

Allow them to decide what and when to share with you. Your task is to be a listening heart. You may continue to ask them, "And what else?" or "Is there anything else?" until they say, "No."

Should they give you several responses, you can say, "I can see where these could really be overwhelming. What is your biggest challenge right now?" For some grievers, this question may take some time to answer as they have been awash in so many things, each of which appears to be demanding their priority attention. Again, ask the question and wait. This is a difficult question to ask of any person; for a person experiencing grief, it can be extremely difficult.

Things that may compound a person's grief beyond the main loss are what are known as secondary losses. For instance, if a wife's husband dies, she may now be faced with having to deal with the finances which he handled. A widower may be faced with cooking meals and shopping. The tasks the partner who died once did are now expected to be done by the living partner. All of these, and others, are changes in the familiar pattern of behavior that had been comfortable and, perhaps, taken for granted. Having to learn new behaviors and the processes necessary to accomplish new tasks simply adds to the grief and stress.

One word of advice. Should a griever give you an answer to this question and follow it up with "What do you think I should do about this?" be cautious. Although you might have a great response about what should be done, be careful not to take control away from the griever. You might say, "I have some ideas, but I would like to know your ideas first." Help the griever look at several options and encourage them to choose one they feel would work. You can then help them with that decision. For instance, if their greatest challenge is in dealing with finances and they decide they need to speak with an accountant, you could recommend one or help them find a good one. Encouraging them to make choices and follow through will help them find a sense of accomplishment and not feel as if they are incompetent.

As grief is primarily an emotional reaction, try to use feeling words in your conversations with a griever. Encourage them to express the emotions they are feeling even if you must ask them, "How is that making you feel right now?" Help them understand that emotions are not permanent. Grief is a mixture of conflicting emotions. Grievers should experience the emotion but not let one emotion define who they are. They are simply experiencing these feelings.

Other factors that may affect a person's grief and their struggle with it may lie in the obvious fact of how quickly life around them is changing. Every day, it seems we are faced with a new challenge or crisis, causing us to adjust our lives. Change is a stressor, and whether wanted or unwanted, it brings experiences of grief and loss. On top of that, the way we have been taught by those around us to handle grief may not be adequate to handle what we are experiencing. John James and Russell Friedman list six major myths that do not help us deal adequately with grief. These include:

1. Don't feel bad. We want to feel good, but grief brings sadness. Many times, grievers are told, "Don't feel bad," although grief is primarily an emotional feeling. The problem comes when grievers translate that to mean don't feel.
2. Replace the loss. When we lose things, our tendency is to simply replace them. That may be easy enough when the loss is related to an object, although even then, grief occurs. When it is a relationship that ends or changes, it becomes much harder. Unless we deal with it adequately, we never really give ourselves to a new relationship.
3. Be strong for others. Occasionally following a death, someone in the family is either told to be strong for others or they simply take it upon themselves to be the rock upon which others can lean. Inadvertently, the message or the action may cause a griever to bury their own grief. This only adds to the pressure within and may cause problems for them later.
4. It takes time. It may be true that time lessens the intensity of some things, but there are many grievers whose loved ones have died 20,

30, or more years ago that, at times, still feel their grief as strongly as ever. Time alone will not heal grief any more than time alone will heal a broken bone. Yes, time will heal a bone, but unless it is set correctly, it will not heal in a functional way. There are steps grievers can take to help them move beyond their loss and live with energy and purpose.
5. Grieve alone. Many people feel uncomfortable around those who grieve and may pull away from those who are grieving. Because grievers tend to withdraw and isolate, many times, they will retreat to quiet places to grieve in order not to disturb others. Sometimes, this myth may also cause grievers to act like they are not grieving and try to meet the happy expectations of those around them. This takes a lot of energy away from that needed to grieve. In your interactions with a grieving person, allow them permission to grieve and express their grief to you without apology.
6. Keep busy. This is one of the biggest myths. People believe if they can stay busy and occupied with other tasks, their grief will fade. While it is true our minds can redirect our emotions, no one can stay busy 24/7. At some point in a busy schedule, there will come a time of quietness. At those times, or when a person lies down to sleep, grief will come rushing back.

As you talk with a griever whose loved one has died, much of the conversation may involve that person. This may be a result of the review they are going through in their minds. Encourage them to talk. Through this process, a person is trying to make sense of what has happened and what they need to do as they piece together the narrative of their life and the relationships they have had.

Dr. Robert A. Neimeyer suggested one way to do this is to list the losses that come to mind about the relationship, but perhaps even others that have occurred in the life of the griever. Another suggestion was to journal daily. In this, a griever may express the things that could have been different not only from the standpoint of the one who has died but also from themselves.

Through journaling, a griever might write statements of apology for things they may have said or done or not said and done. They might write statements of forgiveness for things the other person may have said or done or not said and done. Even statements expressing deep emotional feelings could be written. According to Dr. Robert Neimeyer, journaling even 20 minutes a day leads to healing and moving through a person's grief.

Chapter 11

Helping the Griever Move Forward

With all the writing, discussion, and theorizing about grief, when the experience engulfs us personally, or those we care about, what we really need to see is help with skin on. Grief is not only an overwhelming emotion; it is a daily interaction that affects who we are and the meaning of our life. The Bible is our guide to finding examples and mentors who experienced grief and what we can learn from them. Although we have talked about the supposed Stages of Grief (Denial, Anger, Bargaining, Depression, and Acceptance), I will use that framework to consider the responses to the examples mentioned here.

One of the most well-known examples would be Job. A man who had a good life—wealth, family, and reputation (Job 1:1–5). Although he lost many of them due to circumstances unlike ours, he still suffered losses. Consider some of them which might be the same as us.

1. Wealth—Job 1:13–17
2. Family members—Job 1:18–19
3. Health—Job 2:7–8
4. Reputation and respect—Job 19:9, 13–19

Job, like nearly every other griever, did not deny what had happened.

Job 1:21—*naked I came from my mother's womb and naked I shall return there. The Lord gave and the Lord has taken away*

Job 2:10—*shall we accept good from God and not accept adversity?*

One of the tasks of grief is to recognize the loss, which most grievers have done.

I believe Job, like some grievers, did express anger. Job 7:11—*I will not restrain my mouth; I will speak in the anguish of my spirit, I will complain in the bitterness of my soul.*

Instead of bargaining, Job, like most grievers, simply wanted to make sense of or find meaning in what was happening. Job 2:34—*I would present my case before Him and fill my mouth with arguments …*

Like most grievers, and us as well, Job had expectations of life. Perhaps one of Job's expectations was that if we do good (live like we are supposed to live), things will generally go well. Loss and the accompanying grief seem to shake that expectation. Job 4:7–8—*Remember now, whoever perished being innocent? O where were the upright destroyed? According to what I have seen, those who plow iniquity and those who sow trouble harvest it.*

Although Job could not make sense of what was happening, he was certain God did and that, ultimately, it would be understandable. I do not think Job threw up his hands and said, "Well, I guess I'll just have to live with it." He wanted to have it make sense, and he struggled with the questions he could not answer. However, he was willing to accept that there was One who had the answer, and it would one day be revealed. That hope was based upon a faith in that One before Job's troubles had come. Hear him say in Job 13:15—*though He slay me I will hope in Him.*

A great story to be sure, but the question is, "What can we learn from it, for sojourners and grievers alike?"

For sojourners, perhaps we can learn the following lessons.

1. Grief is not assuaged by logic and intellectual argument, especially if the perception of the griever is that it might partly be their fault. This type of explanation (answering "Why?") only helps to alienate the griever. Don't try to "fix" the griever!
2. Listen to the griever; don't just wait for your turn to speak— Job 21:2. *Listen carefully to my speech, and let this be your way of consolation.*
3. Provide loving support for the griever and do not add to their pain.
4. Sojourners can only support and sustain; God restores. The sojourner cannot be a proxy for the griever.

Lessons for the griever might include:

1. Grief is a normal and natural reaction to loss.
2. Understand that intellectual answers alone do not provide the healing desired. (Would it hurt less if you had all the answers?)
3. Struggle but remain open to the presence of God.

Another example of a griever in Scripture is Jesus. He is sometimes called the Man of Sorrows. Isaiah 53:3 reminds us that *He was despised and forsaken of men, a man of sorrows and acquainted with grief; and like one from whom men turn their face, He was despised, and we did not esteem Him.*

The losses Jesus sustained fall into the category of intangible losses, not the tangible loss of a loved one—although that did happen in the case of Lazarus in John 11. Grief can be caused by things that happen to us, such as rejection or lack of understanding about what we are doing.

Jesus was rejected by:

1. His own people.
    - John 1:11—*He came to His own and those who were His own did not receive Him.*

- Matthew 23:37—*Jerusalem, Jerusalem, who kills the prophets and stones those who are sent to her! How often I wanted to gather your children together the way a hen gathers her chicks under her wings and you were unwilling.*
- They were rejecting Him because of what He was doing in relationship to what they believed was right—John 5:16—*for this reason the Jews were persecuting Jesus because He was doing these things on the Sabbath.*
2. By His hometown—Mark 6:1–6
3. Even by His family—John 7:5—*for not even His brothers were believing in Him.*

Even His coming into this world as a human being, giving up all He had known (Philippians 2:5–8), can be seen as a grief event. As we defined grief early on, it is the conflicting feelings due to a change in or an end of familiar behavior patterns. On top of that, those closest to Him misunderstood what He was about, what He was teaching, and, at times, seemed to work against Him.

- Matthew 15:16—*are you still lacking in understanding also?*
- Mark 4:13—*do you not understand this parable? How will you understand all the parables?*
- Matthew 16:21–23—*From that time Jesus began to show His disciples that He must go to Jerusalem, and suffer many things from the elders and chief priests and scribes, and be killed, and be raised up on the third day. Peter took Him aside and began to rebuke Him saying, "God forbid it, Lord! This shall never happen to You." But He turned and said to Peter, "Get behind Me, Satan! You are a stumbling block to Me; for you are not setting your mind on God's interests, but man's."*

The lessons here are for both sojourners and grievers.

1. There is a time to be alone, just as Jesus spent time alone.
2. Allow people to minister to you—Luke 8:1–3; Matthew 27:55; Mark 15:40; Mark 14:8
3. Even through the pain and isolation, trust in God and His healing.

    a. Hebrews 5:7—*in the days of His flesh He offered up both prayers and supplications with loud crying and tears to the One able to save Him from death and He was heard because of His piety.*
    b. Matthew 26:42 -- *…My Father if this cannot pass away unless I drink it Your will be done.*
    c. This does not guarantee no hurt but a presence to comfort.

I believe the apostle Paul is also an example of a griever. Like Jesus, he suffered some intangible losses that affected his whole being. There was apparently a loss of physical function or health as he described the *thorn in the flesh* he suffered (2 Corinthians 12:7-8). Paul lost his status among his peers, as seen in his journey toward Damascus with the blessing of the Jewish leaders and others, but which soon turned into a plot to kill him because of his conversion (Acts 9:1-2, 23-24). He was also rejected, as seen by various episodes on his missionary journeys and even as he approached the Christians in Jerusalem (Acts 9:26). There was a loss of security as evidenced by his description of shipwrecks, dangers from robbers, danger from his own countrymen and others in 2 Corinthians 11:25-27.

There are some things we can learn from Paul related to grief. These include:

1. Grief will come as a normal and natural result of losses in life.
2. Like Job, hold to the promises of the One who has been your foundation before these things have happened—2 Corinthians 12: 10—*Therefore I am well content with weaknesses, with insults, with distresses, with persecutions, with difficulties, for Christ's sake; for when I am weak, then I am strong.*
3. In all that the griever may experience, never let go of hope.
4. Use the support of those around you, sharing their presence and listening ears. Paul enjoyed the association with people who helped him in physical and emotional ways, as seen by his letters to Christians with whom he had ministered and prayed and who had ministered to and prayed for him.

What takes us through the wilderness of grief and to help those grieve? Primarily, it is the courage to use grief as the process it is that allows us to wrestle our way through the hurt of the losses we face. We must also acknowledge it as an unwanted gift from God that should be used rather than avoided. Grief also helps us to realize our need for others. Let us courageously face our own grief and share the comfort and strength we have found with those around us.

Psalm 30:5—*Weeping may last for the night, but a shout of joy comes in the morning.*

Isaiah 40:28–31—*Do you not know? Have you not heard? The Everlasting God, the Lord, the Creator of the ends of the earth does not become weary or tired. His understanding is inscrutable. He gives strength to the weary, and to him who lacks might He increases power. Though youths grow weary and tired, and vigorous young men stumble badly, yet those who wait for the Lord will gain new strength; they will mount up with wings like eagles, they will run and not get tired, they will walk and not become weary.*

Chapter 12

Ministering to a Family Following a Suicide

Ministering to grieving families is often difficult. There are those occasions when the loved one who died was a faithful Christian, and the family relations were generally loving. Grief still touches these families, and they will need loving and respectful care shown to them as they move through their grief. Other times, death touches a family who are experiencing struggles and tensions within family relationships. These, too, need care and support in their grief.

One of the most difficult occasions in which you may be called upon to minister is when the death a family is experiencing is the suicide of a loved one. There is a special intensity in situations such as this, as well as the perceived unraveling of a family's structure and understanding of their world. In this setting, you will be called upon like never before to be God's presence—not His voice—to a family needing a solid place upon which to stand. You also must become and be seen as a safe person who will listen without probing or judging. Talk little but listen intently with good active listening skills. Any questions you ask should be open-ended ones that will invite them to speak about and share their feelings and thoughts.

Although we would hope we never have to face it, the statistics remind us that it is an ever-increasing possibility. According to the Center for

Disease Control and Prevention (CDC) website:

- Suicide rates increased 37% between 2000-2018 and decreased 5% between 2018-2020. However, rates nearly returned to their peak in 2021.
- Overall, the number of deaths by suicide increased by 2.6% between 2021 and 2022.
- In 2021, 48,123 people died by suicide in the United States. (That is 1 death every 11 minutes.)
- 3.5 million adults made a plan for suicide.
- 1.7 million adults attempted suicide.

Much could be said about factors possibly leading to such numbers, but if these figures tell us anything, they tell us it is an all-too-common event that people must face. In fact, it is estimated that 85% of people in the United States personally know someone who has died by suicide as suicide is one of the top ten leading causes of death across all age groups.

There is also a sense in which a suicide is different than other deaths. Barbara Coloroso shared this insight:

> One aspect of suicide that sets it apart from other deaths is that the mourners must grieve for the very person who has taken the life of that person. The victim and the villain are one and the same. The decision to die and the no longer being alive occur in the same time and space, to magnify the grief. The mourners feel a deliberate abandonment and rejection, while at the same time they feel an anger and rage. The *whys* and the *what ifs* combine with *How could she do this to us?* and *Why couldn't she come to us?* Mourners can't just experience the piercing grief of good-bye; they get hammered by these questions and hammered by the reality that they belong to a different group of mourners than any they have ever been a part of before.

The five S's, unbidden and unwelcome, arrive to sit squarely in the living room, daring anyone to speak their names and shatter their presence. It is only in speaking their names and shattering their presence that the mourners can get on with their grieving. Stigma, shame, secrets, silence, and sin can remain only if those of us who grieve do so silently, feeling shame, afraid to speak the unspeakable word "suicide" and give it its due, but no more, in the life story of the one who has died. We need to speak the person's name, tell his entire life story, and laugh. Laughter helps us to see life's ironies and recognize the larger whole of the story.

It is bad enough that a loved one has died. However, following a suicide, a family may find themselves feeling more isolated and receiving less support than families suffering another death might receive. This is due in part to some of the lingering issues Coloroso called out.

A family experiencing the death of a loved one by suicide may find themselves feeling abandoned by what they consider a familiar support group of friends. Those left behind may also find it difficult to talk to others about their loss because of the discomfort others may feel related to the manner of death. In fact, in a study done in 1980, researchers found that respondents to the survey indicated that parents of a child who died by suicide are viewed as:

- Less likable
- More to blame
- More ashamed
- More able to have prevented the death

It may be this carryover stigma from generations past creates a double-edged sword for those in this setting. They may find themselves trying to hide the cause of death from others and feeling ashamed for something over which they had no real control. This shame may initiate feelings of guilt, wondering what signs or signals they missed that might have stopped the death from occurring.

As mentioned earlier, they may feel abandoned and rejected by those whose support is sought. Thus, these grievers retreat into the silence of loneliness, deepening their grief. As the body of Christ, we are to *Rejoice with those who rejoice and weep with those who weep,* as Paul exhorts us in Romans 12:15. There are no restrictions or exclusions in that exhortation. Grievers need support, especially from those who share many of the same values and faith as themselves.

Another carryover issue that may enter into this scenario is the belief that the taking of one's own life is a sin and thus condemning that person to hell. There have been, and are, some religious groups who espouse this belief in word and practice. I do not know what your particular view is on this, but I am of the opinion this is some bad theology. In Appendix 1, there is a study of suicide for you to consider. No matter what your personal beliefs are related to this form of death and the eternal destination of the one who dies by suicide, it does not help the family with their grief to have someone tell them their loved one is in hell.

One of *the* strongest emotions you may encounter in this type of setting is anger. Grievers will be angry at the person who took their own life, feeling that this person had rejected them or abandoned them. This is a double hurt if they are also feeling that way about a support group that does not show up for them. Grievers may be angry at other family members, feeling they are ignoring or dismissing the death because of the manner in which it occurred. If the person who died was in therapy or had been seeing a mental health professional, there may be anger directed toward that person for not seeing the signs.

Above all else, grievers may direct their anger toward God, which can also lead to a crisis of faith. They may question the goodness of God in letting their loved one do this act. They will be asking *WHY?*, expecting God to help them make sense out of it. For the most part, there will never be answers. The one person who could explain it is now dead. It is not your place to answer for God. The only thing that can honestly be said is, "I don't know, but God is here in this." It may also be that a better question to ask is *Now what? What do I do with my loved one's suicide?* For this question there can be an answer if the person is willing to seek it.

If I may venture one thought. Many times, death by suicide is seen as a very selfish act where the person who kills themselves does not seem to be thinking of what their actions may do to those they love. If, however, a person is feeling so much pain and hopelessness, they may feel they are being a burden on those who love them and feel that if they were out of the picture, others would be better off. Therefore, to them, their actions may be, in their mind, an act of love. I do not mean to dismiss the pain that causes such a decision or the pain it causes those left behind. I just wonder if this option would reframe much of the negative emotion and struggle attendant in this setting.

You may have noticed in this discussion I have not said *committed suicide*, which is usually how we hear it or say it. I believe it is better to be careful with our language. Although it is not meant this way, sometimes when we use the phrase *committed suicide*, it may subconsciously be heard as we talk about bad things like *he committed a crime*. Could it be that such language adds to the shame and stigma of suicide?

Going back to ministering to families in this setting, remember to be that safe person who can listen without judgment or pulling back because of your own discomfort. As you listen, grievers will tell you what they need to say and help you direct them toward healing. Listening to their story honors them and their loved one. However, do not force them to talk until they are ready. Encourage them to express their emotions. When speaking, do not discount what they are saying. Statements like *Well, at least…* or *However…* may undermine what the griever wants to say and cause them to retreat from you.

When you talk with them, you do not always have to start with *"How are you doing?"* You probably know the answer to that. Help them think and express their feelings. Ask: *What has been the most difficult thing for you in this? What has changed for you over the last week* (or other time period)?

Here are some basic things that you should do and avoid.

Do

- Accept that you may feel awkward or uncomfortable talking about suicide. You can even admit that you don't know what to say or do. Just don't let your discomfort keep you from reaching out.
- Invite the person to talk about the loved one they've lost or share memories—if that's what they want to do. The important thing is to be there, whether the person needs a shoulder to cry on or a listening ear.
- Understand that they may have many strong and conflicting emotions at this time. There is no right or wrong way to feel or behave after a loss to suicide—so allow the person to express their pain and loss without judgment.
- Offer to help with practical tasks, such as grocery shopping, preparing meals, notifying others of the death, or helping with funeral arrangements, for example.
- Use terms such as "died by suicide," "took their life," or "chose to end their life" when talking about the person's death.

Don't

- Use the term "committed suicide". This implies that suicide is a criminal act and will only reinforce the stigma and make the grieving person feel more isolated.
- Make judgments about the person who died or label them as weak, selfish, or crazy, for example. Suicide is the result of extreme emotional distress, not a character defect.
- Demand an explanation or speculate on why the person took their own life. Your role is to be supportive, not to interrogate the person grieving. Listen and allow them to direct the conversation.
- Issue platitudes such as "they're at peace now" or "they're in a better place." Such shallow reassurances rarely provide comfort and can even alienate the grieving person, making them feel more alone.
- Lose patience. Someone grieving a suicide may need to talk about their loss over and over again without fear of interruption or

judgment. Talking over the same points can help them come to terms with what happened.

Help the grievers to set good boundaries about the people they choose to draw near to and the actions they take. Remind them that their grief journey is unique and should not be directed by anyone else. Encourage them, however, to let others into their life again, perhaps joining a support group. Help them extend grace to themselves and to others. Encourage them to maintain good eating, sleeping, and exercise habits. If needed, help them restore their spiritual faith.

The manner of death may cause those left behind to have good memories about the deceased; it is important for them to remember that person and the relationship with honesty. There is good and bad in every relationship. However, when a person dies, we sometimes paint them as having done nothing good or nothing bad. Honesty about the ups and downs and the feelings those things engendered within us helps in the healing process.

Perhaps one of the biggest factors related to our healing from this kind of event is forgiveness. Forgiveness is not simply wiping it away as it never happened, nor is it minimizing what it did to us. Forgiveness is the decision to not hold it as a tool to hurt another. Such forgiveness is a process, not a one-time decision or statement. In remembering things about the deceased that may have hurt you as a griever, forgiveness is choosing not to let that thing hurt you any longer by forgiving the deceased or by saying it out loud to the deceased. In helping the griever work through this, you who minister to them will be helping them heal.

Chapter 13

Ministering to a Family After the Death of a Child

Ministering to a family following the death of a child, especially stillbirths or miscarriages, is perhaps one of the most heart-wrenching tasks you may be called upon to do. People expect older adults to die, but not children. It seems to especially upset the natural order of things when a baby dies. Although much of what has been said to this point is applicable, this is a time for simply being present with those who are hurting.

The death of a baby or child brings about very intense emotions for parents. This is a profound loss, and parents need to grieve the loss. Unfortunately, the death of a child or baby is many times minimized by our society. Other people seem to assume that if it was a miscarriage, the couple will probably have more children as time moves on. If it is the death of a child, many will think the same thing, or if the family has other children, that these children will help the parents cope with the loss. Both reactions neglect to deal with and care for the current and personal loss that is felt.

Let's first consider a couple who has suffered a miscarriage. Later, we will move to dealing with the death of a child.

According to WebMD, miscarriages are common. However, it's hard to know exactly how often they occur because many times, it is before a woman even knows she is pregnant. About 10-20% of recognized pregnancies will end in a miscarriage, but researchers estimate the overall rate is closer to 40%. Therefore, there is a good chance that you will be called upon to minister in this type of loss.

As discussed earlier, grief overwhelms us. Mentally, there is a shift from our rational thinking part of the brain (the frontal cortex) to the amygdala, which has a lot to do with our emotions. There is also a disconnect between the two hemispheres of the brain, which causes emotions to move to the forefront of our thinking and actions without the governing aspect of our thinking to help slow the emotions.

In this emotional overload, there is a strong feeling of failure, especially on the mother's part. Deborah Davis wrote, "A sense of inadequacy, particularly for mothers, may arise from the idea that your body betrayed you, or that you are less of a woman or less of a mother because your baby died."

Along with the feeling of inadequacy may come the feelings of anger and guilt. These feelings may arise because they reinforce our belief that we are in control of what happens to us. The death of a baby, along with most other tragedies, confronts us with the idea that we are not in control. You may be facing a mother or both parents holding on to these feelings to avoid the feeling of helplessness that comes with such a loss.

There is the death of the hopes and unrealized dreams that were held and imagined for the child. Even in the short time the child was in the mother's womb, each parent had envisioned the days and years to come and what would or could be done in them. These will be remembered as those anticipated milestones arrive and will touch their lives in the future.

Sadly, there are no cultural norms for mourning the loss of someone who never lived outside the womb and was never formally welcomed into the larger community of family and friends. Family friends and even family members may make this experience even more difficult by things they say and do. Do not minimize their feelings or cause them to feel guilty for having them. They are normal and natural responses. Help them express their feelings. Deborah Davis said, "It is also important to remember that the only way to work your way through grief is to acknowledge all of your feelings. However painful this may be, it's the only way, and in the long run, acknowledging is actually less harmful than repressing or avoiding grief. In fact, experts in bereavement agree that the quality of your grief work can determine the quality of your life."

This will not be done immediately. Many of the initial emotions are very intense and raw and cannot be expressed fully. Your presence and assurance that what they are feeling is okay will be of great help. Remember, there is no right or wrong way to grieve. Each person expresses and handles grief differently. Do not try to have them fit some *expected* mold of acting.

Do not be offended if they seem to turn away from you or others. Grief causes grievers to isolate. Add to that the feeling of inadequacy or failure and you may be able to understand why folks suffering this kind of tragedy do not want others around. Be a safety barrier for them as you may need to run interference between them and other well-wishers. Do not keep others from them but help them be aware of the emotions that they may encounter.

Things that are NOT helpful to say are:
1. You are still healthy; you can have other children.
2. There must have been something wrong with the child. Perhaps this is a good thing.
3. At least your baby is with God and won't have to face the pitfalls of this world.

A part of your ministry of presence will include your walking with them through some difficult but important decisions regarding a stillbirth.
1. Whether the parents, especially the mother, want to see the body. Deborah Davis said many times, the baby's body will not be shown

to the mother for fear of upsetting her. It is her feeling, however, that for the mother to see the body validates the existence of the child that lived inside of her. Help the parents work through their feelings on this.

2. What is to be done with the body? Will it be cremated or turned over to a funeral home? It is important that some ritual be considered whether it is a funeral involving many people or a simple ceremony involving just the parents and/or immediate families. Don't forget that grandparents and others are also grieving this loss. Kenneth Doka wrote about the importance of ritual by saying, "This rite of passage provides a sense of structure and support in highly stressful times, and a safe venue for the physical and emotional expression of grief."

After a loss such as this, it is normal for people to want information—information about what happened, why, or how to cope with the loss. Encourage the parents to find that information, whether it is asking the doctor, the nurses, or others who might know. Having knowledge, at times, can help us feel less vulnerable. Such information may not provide the answers sought, but it can provide a person with the empowerment they need to deal with life ahead.

One resource for you to consider is other parents who have experienced this same grief event. Talk to them. Find out how they have dealt with this in their lives. You may find out they have not, giving you an opportunity to minister to them as well. If they have found good coping strategies, you might ask if they would talk to the couple presently experiencing the event. If so, you could approach the currently suffering couple to see if they would allow the other couple to visit with them. Make sure you vet the couple who have already gone through the event. You might also see if the couples want you to be present when they meet.

Be aware, however, that feelings of grief can come at unpredictable times, but especially on anniversary dates of the event, holidays, etc. Let the parents know you are available to talk with them any time they need a listening ear or encourage them to find that safe person who will listen.

Just because time passes does not mean the pain or sadness will go away. Help the parents to know and give themselves permission to feel those emotions whenever they need to.

You may also need to encourage the grieving parents to re-engage in activities and not lock themselves away. However, it may be difficult for the woman especially to be part of groups at church with women her own age and their children. Encourage them to share how they feel so they do not drift away from each other. There are a couple of groups who offer resources and help for parents whose babies died. Compassionate Friends (compassionatefriends.org) and Share (share.org) are two of those groups.

If the situation involves an older child, many of the same feelings and emotions will be present, especially for the parents. Therese Rando wrote:

> With the death of their child, a parent feels he or she has failed in the basic function of parenthood: taking care of the children and the family. A parent is supposed to protect and provide for their child. They are supposed to keep her from all harm. She should be the one who grows up healthy to bury her parents ...

The death of any child is a monumental assault on the parents' sense of identity. Because they cannot carry out their role of preserving their own child, they may experience an oppressive sense of failure, a loss of power and ability, and a deep sense of being violated. Disillusionment, emptiness, and insecurity may follow, all of which stem from a diminished sense of self. And this can lead to the guilt, which is a common feature in parental grief.

Again, a key point of your ministry is simply to be there for the parents, helping them to realize they are experiencing normal and natural reactions to what has happened. It is important to help them find ways to express and verbalize what they are feeling in order to process their grief and move through it.

Below is a sampling of Bible verses you might find helpful. Do not make promises like, "This verse will help you." Instead, use language like, "Here is a verse you might consider and see if it gives you anything to think about."

Psalm 34:18—*the Lord is near to the brokenhearted and saves those who are crushed in spirit.*

Psalm 46:1–5—*God is our refuge and strength, a very present help in trouble. Therefore we will not fear though the earth should change and the mountains slip into the heart of the sea; though its waters roar and foam, though the mountains quake at its swelling pride. There is a river whose streams make glad the city of God, the holy dwelling places of the Most High. God is in the midst of her, she will not be moved; God will help her when the morning dawns.*

Psalm 56:3—*when I am afraid, I will put my trust in You.*

Psalm 73:26—*my flesh and my heart may fail, but God is the strength of my heart and my portion forever.*

Isaiah 41:10—*Do not fear, for I am with you; do not anxiously look about you, for I am your God. I will strengthen you, surely I will help you, surely I will uphold you with My righteous right hand.*

John 16:33—*These things I have spoken to you, so that in Me you might have peace. In the world you have tribulation, but take courage I have overcome the world.*

2 Corinthians 1:3–5—*Blessed be the God and Father of our Lord Jesus Christ, the Father of mercies and God of all comfort, who comforts us in all our affliction so that we may be able to comfort those who are in any affliction with the comfort with which we ourselves are comforted by God. For just as the sufferings of Christ are ours in abundance, so also our comfort is abundant through Christ.*

Philippians 4:6–7—*Be anxious for nothing, but in everything by prayer and supplication with thanksgiving let your requests be made known to God. And the peace of God, which surpasses all comprehension, will guard your hearts and your minds in Christ Jesus.*

Appendix 1

Introduction

There are a few words that cause apprehension, confusion, and even fear in the hearts and minds of people who hear them, such as cancer. Another of those words is suicide. As those who may be involved in the lives of those touched by this event, we struggle to know how to respond or help. We may feel more powerless when confronted by a person contemplating suicide.

I. SUICIDE IN SCRIPTURE AND HISTORY
   A. In Scripture, we do not find any judgments on suicide, only recorded instances.
      1. Old Testament
         a. Abimelech—Judges 9:54
         b. Samson—Judges 16:28–31
         c. Saul—1 Kings 31:1-6
         d. Saul's armor-bearer—2 Chronicles 10:5
         e. Ahithophel—2 Samuel 17:23
         f. Zimri—1 Kings 16:18
      2. New Testament—Judas—Matthew 27:3–5
      3. Extra-biblical—Jews at Masada

   B. Church history
      1. Augustine—thought suicide was generally unlawful and indicative of a weak mind.
      2. Council of Arles—452 AD/CE—was the first religious conclave to condemn suicide.
      3. 2nd Council of Orleans—533 AD/CE—ordered that offerings and oblations be refused for suicides.
      4. Council of Brage—563 AD/CE—denied burial rites at the burial of suicides.
      5. Council of Toledo—693 AD/CE—punished suicide attempts with exclusion from church fellowship for 2 months.

6. In the 1200s, Thomas Aquinas said the commandment not to kill included oneself as well as others.

C. During the Middle Ages, civil law began to follow church teaching and practice.
1. Desecration of the corpse of suicides became standard practice.
   a. The body was dragged into the street
   b. A stake was driven through the heart
   c. The body was then left unburied at a crossroads or hung from a gallows to rot
   d. The last body dragged into the streets in England was in 1823.

2. Suicide was surrounded by superstition and fear
   a. If the suicide was in a house, the body had to be taken out through a window or a portion of a wall had to be removed.
   b. In Scotland, a suicide could not be buried in sight of the sea or cultivated land or fishing or farming would be harmed.
3. In 1882, England ruled suicides could have normal burials, but a strong feeling and reaction continues.

II. REASONS FOR SUICIDE
A. Definition: suicide is a deliberate act of self-destruction in which the chance of survival is uncertain.

B. The best reason is psychological pain or *psychache*. Here is a description by Edwin Schneidman, founder of the American Association of Suicidology.

Psychache is the hurt, anguish, or ache that takes hold in the mind. It is intrinsically psychological—the pain of excessively felt shame, guilt, fear, anxiety, loneliness, angst, dread of growing old or dying badly. When psychache occurs, its introspective reality is undeniable. Suicide happens when the psychache is deemed unbearable, and death is actively sought to stop the unceasing flow of painful consciousness. Suicide is a tragic drama in the mind.

C. Dr. Schneidman placed the psychological needs not being met in people who commit suicidal acts into the following five (5) areas:

1. Some take their life because their need for love, acceptance and belonging has been thwarted.
2. Some people's needs for control, predictability, and arrangement have been fractured, which are related to their needs for achievement, autonomy, order, and understanding, which also are not met.
3. Some feel their self-image has actually been assaulted; they are trying to avoid shame, defeat, humiliation, or disgrace; they don't feel any affiliation.
4. Some people's key relationships have been ruptured, which is often tied into frustrated needs of nurturance and affirmation.
5. Some have excessive anger, rage, and hostility—when this occurs, you often have a person whose need for dominance and aggression has been blocked.

D. H. Norman Wright described four (4) other patterns of suicide.

1. Suicidal depression: a person is sitting on a high level of unacceptable rage that has developed because of a series of events in life over which they have no control.
2. Relief of pain: people with a low threshold for pain and who experience chronic pain can be candidates for suicide. The death of a family member or friend causes too much pain.
3. Revenge: Some people feel overwhelmed by hurt or rejection from another person. Their desire to hurt back is stronger than their desire to live.

4. Hopelessness: About 25% of those committing suicide do so after much thought, considering the pros and cons of living and dying. For them, death seems to be the better option. Others, such as those with serious illness and/or age, do not want to be a burden on others.

IV. MYTHS ASSOCIATED WITH SUICIDE

A. Suicide and attempted suicide are the same kind of behavior.
   1. Suicide is usually committed by someone who wants to die; attempted suicide is generally done as a cry for help in order to go on living.
   2. Some folks plan a suicide attempt, not wanting to die, but nevertheless do.

B. Suicide is a problem of a specific class of people.
   1. Suicide touches all classes, ages and gender of people.
   2. There are, however, statistical tendencies showing those at greater risk.

C. People who talk about suicide don't commit suicide.
   1. About 80% of those who commit suicide have communicated their intention to do so to someone prior to doing it. However, some of the indications are not fully recognized until after it has happened.
   2. Ignoring a person who talks about suicide isn't the best solution. Threatening suicide should always be taken seriously. It is a very important warning signal. There may be cases where that's all it is, but no one should make that assumption, even if it was just an attention-getter. How do you ever know that?

D. Once a person is suicidal, they are suicidal forever: Not true. Many who have thought of or attempted suicide have discovered the answers to their problems, have moved on, and are no longer suicidal.

E. Suicide is inherited or runs in families.
   1. Although not scientifically proven ...
      a. Suicide committed by a family member now puts that option into a person's frame of reference.
      b. Some families seem to pass on a genetic susceptibility to depression or other mental disorders which can lead to suicidal thoughts.
      c. The family member's suicide may create depression in other family members.
   2. However, today's stress levels affect everyone, no matter what the family history may be.

F. A Christian will not commit suicide: Not true. Christians are human like everyone else and can allow life to cloud their faith.

G. Suicide and depression are synonymous: there are folks who suffer with depression who do not have suicidal thoughts.

H. Improvement after a suicidal crisis means the risk of suicide is over.
   1. A study by the Los Angeles Suicide Prevention Center indicated that almost half of those who had been in a suicidal crisis actually committed suicide within three (3) months of passing through their first crisis.

   2. If a person immediately states that their problems are solved and seems to be overly happy after a suicidal crisis, those close to them should be concerned.

Conclusion

Most people who attempt suicide don't actually want to die; they want out of their suffering. Their pain is so great that they don't see any solution to stop it other than death. They are usually alone with their own mind filled with depression that tells them not only is their life horrible now, but it's always been horrible, and it will never change. It is the depression doing that talking and distorting reality.

Appendix 2

Steps for the Sojourning Process

Ask the grieving person if they would like to meet regularly to talk about their loss or upcoming loss.

A. Meet as often as needed but have agreed upon limits.

B. Schedule the time and place for the meeting.
    1. Knowing there is a time to meet may help the griever feel connected.
    2. Make sure the place is private enough for the griever to express their feelings openly.

C. During the meeting, stay on the subject of their loss or grief; do not wander off just to talk or to avoid the pain of their grief.

D. Encourage the griever to use "I" messages when sharing their feelings. (I feel sad; not this has caused me sadness.)

E. Help and encourage the griever to honestly express their feelings and thoughts. Create a safe harbor for them to do this without expressing shock or judgment.

F. Do not try to make the person feel better or fix them; just be there and listen.

G. Allow the griever to cry—without apologizing to you.

H. If you do share some of your experiences, keep it short.

I. Allow for "time-outs" if needed. If the time limit is reached, say, "I need to go now, but let's pick up here next time." Do not leave them feeling abandoned.

J. Help the person identify and name any needs that need to be addressed and/or may need help accomplishing.

K. Explore with the person ways these needs can be met.

L. Hold to the agreed time limits but set the next meeting before parting.

M. Make sure you, as a sojourner, have a way to release any pain you may have absorbed during the meeting so that your energy, etc., can be maintained.

Appendix 3

Grief and Assessment

News headlines and reports speak to us about death nearly every day. Whether it is a well-known person or people unknown to us, a single death or a multiple-death event, the presence of death in this world cannot be denied. It can, however, be ignored.

By that, I mean that although death permeates our consciousness, it does not often enter our conversations—especially the bereavement and grief which death brings. We seem to have the child-like attitude that if something is not talked about, it doesn't exist. Anthropologist Margaret Mead is reported to have said, "When a person is born, we rejoice; when they are married, we jubilate; but when they die, we try to pretend that nothing happened."

It is interesting to note that faith and doubt can co-exist. For instance, in Luke 7:18-23 it is recorded that while John the Baptist was in prison, he sent two of his disciples to Jesus to ask Him, "Are you the Expected One, or do we look for another?" This is the same John who, in John 1:33-34 spoke of his experience in baptizing Jesus by saying he had seen the dove descending on Jesus, which was the sign he had been given to know who the Son of God was. However, Jesus was not necessarily acting as John thought the Messiah would act, so he sent his followers to confirm what he had seen.

Sometimes, a person experiencing grief begins to question some of their beliefs. In fact, it is sometimes during grief that bad theology is discovered. Therefore, it is of utmost importance to have patience with those who are struggling with faith during their grief. Create a safe and sacred place where a griever can share their story with you and begin to find healing.

I want to share some thoughts that may help you minister to those in grief, especially when grief turns into a crisis of faith.

I. BASICS
   A. Definition of bereavement & grief
      1. Bereavement: the state or fact of being bereaved (suffering the death of a loved one)

      2. Grief:

         a. The normal and natural emotional reaction to loss of any kind.
         b. The conflicting feelings caused by the end of or change in a familiar pattern of behavior.
         c. Grief, then, is the response to bereavement.

   B. People experiencing grief are NOT living from their head, but rather their heart.
      1. Normal person & division between head & heart
      2. Normal person with grief events that had been dealt with
      3. Ashley Davis Bush described it this way:

> Your journey along the grief road actually began long, long ago, with your very first breath of life…Every day thereafter, you have experienced thousands of minor and major losses—from the loss of a bottle to the loss of a job, from the loss of your baby teeth to the loss of a friendship, from the loss of childhood innocence to the loss of adult dreams.

> Every life transition, every beginning and ending you've ever experienced involved loss...Effectively, they are grieving. Life is full of painful endings not related specifically to death, such as a job loss, an illness, a romantic breakup, or divorce, and each of these also requires a transition stage as the old is discarded and the new is formulated.
>
> So, the truth is that, whether you realize it or not, you've actually been grieving on some level throughout your life. Clearly some losses are more traumatic than others, and some are harder to adapt to, thus requiring more time and energy...That's why understanding the grieving process is critical, since it is a relentless reality approaching every one of us at every turn in life.

    4. Whatever the grief event was, affirm the loss rather than trying to rationalize or minimize it. After a loss, a person's whole theological worldview may be shaken or shattered.

C. The way to move people back is to begin a spiritual conversation.
    1. Hear their story.
    2. Don't try to "fix" them or remake what seems to be a broken or skewed theological framework.
    3. Suppose that when you try to begin a spiritual conversation they say, "I'm spiritual, but not religious." You might respond by saying, "You know, Jesus didn't appear to be that religious either, at least as the religious people saw it. What do you mean by saying you are spiritual?"
    4. Engage them with broad questions.
        a. What are the sources of hope and comfort for you?
        b. How have you found these to help you cope in the past?
        c. What are some of the religious or spiritual needs you have?

II. SPIRITUAL ASSESSMENT TOOL
   A. The Spiritual Core
      1. Intersection of human and divine relationships
      2. Here you find...
         a. What a person treasures
         b. What gives a person meaning and hope
         c. These are the things that may be most shaken during grief
      3. Questions to ask
         a. What is most important to you?
         b. What gives you guidance and direction?
         c. What gives you strength and motivates you?
         d. What gives you meaning and hope?

   B. Relationships—divine and human
      1. Vertical (divine) and horizontal (human) relationships are closely intertwined.
      2. Listen and look for...
         a. Connections—along the human relationship plane
         b. Sources of strength
         c. Wounds/conflicts
         d. Ambivalence
      2. Relationship questions
         a. When do you feel the most connected to God?
         b. When do you feel the most connected to other people?
         c. What relationships make you feel safe?
         d. What relationships bring you comfort and nurture you?

   C. Faith development
      1. What events or people have influenced their faith?
      2. Questions to ask:
         a. What did you learn from these events/people?
         b. What has changed for you because of those events?
         c. Who are the most positive influences on your faith journey?

D. Faith perception
   1. Sometimes, a person's perception of faith changes in the midst of trauma and/or grief.
   2. Questions to ask:
      a. How has your perception of faith changed over the years?
      b. Would you describe your relationship with God more as a head or a heart relationship?
      c. How do you believe God interacts with the world?

E. Faith practice
   1. The way a person practices or lives out their faith may change through the years or in a time of trauma/grief.
   2. Questions to ask:
      a. How has the way you live out your faith changed over the years?
      b. What religious or faith practices do you find most comforting and energizing?
      c. When do you feel most connected/disconnected to God in your faith?

F. Faith dissonance
   1. Sometimes, this may be the place you start because it is here a person who is hurting may be struggling.
   2. Be aware that you may often be the brunt of their hurt because they may perceive you as the link to God or the church—don't take it personally.
   3. Questions to ask
      a. What are you struggling with the most right now in your faith?
      b. What other hurts or questions about faith and/or God do you have that this brings up?

Conclusion

Working with people in grief provides a unique opportunity to help them re-affirm their faith or to grow their faith in a heavenly Father who cares. Grief is a journey they will travel for the rest of their lives. However, in the midst of it, God is there and intertwines Himself in their lives (Psalm 42:1-11).

May God bless you in your ministry!

Spiritual Assessment Tool for Crises and Grief

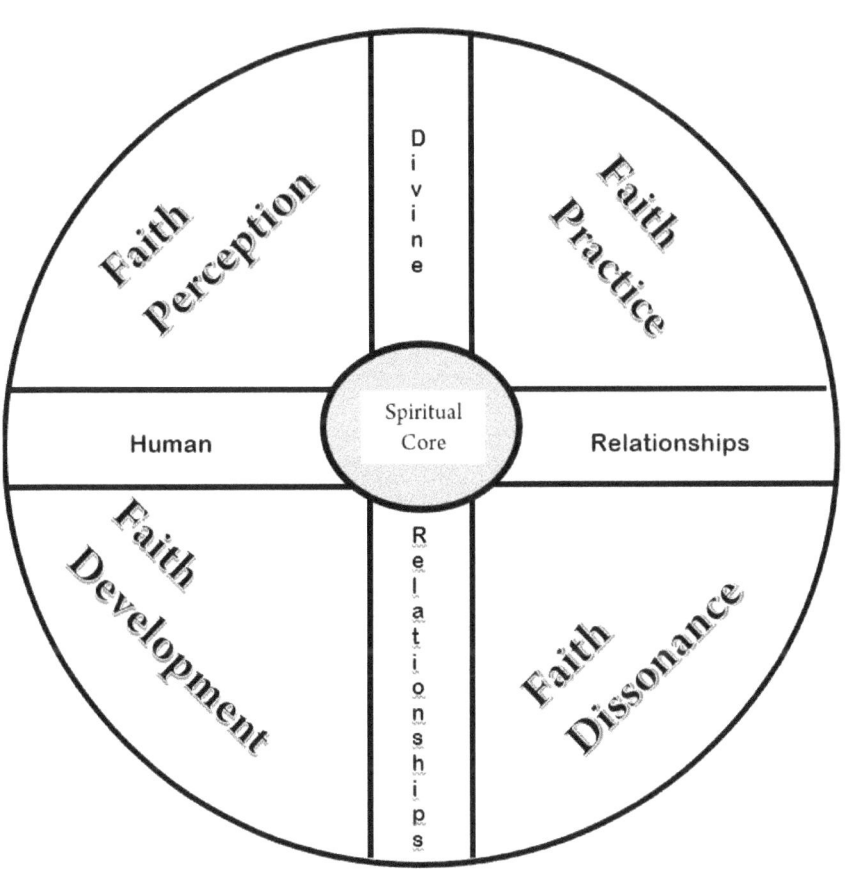

Appendix 4

A Guide for Those Helping Others with Grief

Don't try to find the magic words or formula to eliminate the pain. Nothing can erase or minimize the painful tragedy your friend or loved one is facing. Your primary role at this time is simply to "be there." Don't worry about what to say or do, just be a presence that the person can lean on when needed.

Don't try to minimize or make the person feel better. When we care about someone, we hate to see them in pain. Often, we will say things like, "I know how you feel," or "Perhaps it was for the best" in order to minimize their hurt. While this can work in some instances, it never works with grief.

Help with responsibilities. Even though a life has stopped, life doesn't. One of the best ways to help is to run errands, prepare food, take care of the kids, do laundry and help with the simplest maintenance.

Don't expect the person to reach out to you. Many people say, "Call me if there is anything I can do." At this stage, the person who is grieving will be overwhelmed at the simple thought of picking up a phone. If you are close to this person, simply drop over and begin to help. People need this but don't think to ask. There are many people that will be with you during the good times—but few that are there in life's darkest hour.

Talk through decisions. While working through the grief process, many grievers report difficulty with decision-making. Be a sounding board for your friend or loved one and help them think through decisions. Don't be afraid to ask them, "Have you thought about this option?" or "How do you think that will turn out in the long run?"

Don't be afraid to say the name of the deceased. Those who have lost someone usually speak of them often, and believe it or not, need to hear the deceased's name and stories. In fact, many grievers welcome this.

Remember that time does not heal all wounds. Your friend or loved one will change because of what has happened. Everyone grieves differently. Some will be "fine" and then experience their true grief a year later; others grieve immediately. There are **NO** timetables and **NO** rules. Be patient.

Remind the griever to take care of themselves. Eating, resting and self-care are all difficult tasks when besieged by the taxing emotions of grief. You can help by keeping the house stocked with healthy foods that are already prepared or easy to prepare. Help them with maintenance tasks. However, do not push the griever to do things they may not be ready to do. Many grievers say, "I wish they would just follow my lead." While it may be upsetting to see the griever withdrawing from people and activities—it is normal. They will rejoin when they are ready.

Avoid judging. Don't tell the griever how to react or handle their emotions or situation. Simply let them know that you support their decisions and will help them in what needs doing. Share a meal. Invite the griever over regularly to share a meal or take it to their house since meal times can be especially lonely. Consider inviting the griever out on important dates like the one-month anniversary of the death, the deceased's birthday, or holidays.

Make a list of everything that needs to be done with the griever. This could include bill paying to plant watering. Prioritize them by importance. Help the griever complete as many tasks as possible. If there are many responsibilities, find one or more additional friends to support and help you.

Make a personal commitment to help the grieving person through this time in their life. After a death, many friendships change or disintegrate. People don't know how to relate to the grieving person, or they get tired of being around someone who is sad. Vow to see your friend or loved one through this, to be their anchor in their darkest hour.

Bibliography / Resources

Deborah L. Davis, Ph.D., *Empty Cradle, Broken Heart* (Golden, CO: Fulcrum Publishing), 1996.

Kenneth Doka, *Grief Is a Journey* (New York: Atria Paperback), 2016.

John James and Russell Friedman, *The Grief Recovery Handbook, 20th Anniversary Expanded Edition* (New York: HarperCollins), 2009.

Junietta Baker McCall, *Bereavement Counseling* (New York: Routledge), 2004.

Brook Noel and Pamela D. Blair, Ph.D. *I Wasn't Ready to Say Good-bye: A Guide for Surviving, Coping and Healing after the Sudden Death of a Loved One* (Milwaukee: Champion Press), 2000.

Ester Shapiro, *Grief As A Family Process* (New York: Guildford Press), 1995.

Tim VanDuivendyk, *The Unwanted Gift of Grief* (New York: The Haworth Press, Inc.) 2006.

H. Norman Wright, *The Complete Guide to Crisis & Trauma Counseling* (Minneapolis: Bethany House), 2011.

_____, *Helping Those in Grief* (Ventura, CA: Regal), 2011.

_____, *Helping Those Who Hurt* (Minneapolis: Bethany House), 2003.

Living with Grief, Kenneth J. Doka, editor. (Washington, DC: Hospice Foundation of America), 2002.

Other information related to grieving and helping those in grief can be found at the website for the Grief Recovery Institute of Bend, Oregon. There are articles related to grief and a directory of trained Grief Recovery Specialists who can help people work through the Grief Recovery Method. That web address is:

www.griefrecoverymethod.com

A Google search will also uncover other organizations that help those in grief.

www.ingramcontent.com/pod-product-compliance
Lightning Source LLC
Chambersburg PA
CBHW041926090426
42743CB00020B/3453